FOOTBALL
FAMILY

FOOTBALL FAMILY

The Story of Jim Algeo and the Rare Breed of Lansdale Catholic

M. Bridget Algeo

Foreword by Mike Stern

Print ISBN: 978-1-54397-391-4

eBook ISBN: 978-1-54397-392-1

Dedicated to my parents,
Big Jim & Mick

TABLE OF CONTENTS

Foreword

By Mike Stern

Be prepared to laugh. Be prepared to cry. Be prepared to celebrate life and faith. Be prepared to love.

Whether you are a young student, a grizzled athletics coach or administrator, a loving, caring mom or dad, or someone who plays or enjoys football or any other sport, your heart will be caressed as you read this story about a very special family and the multitude of students and athletes whom their lives touched.

Football Family is a well-paced memoir about a special family – the Algeos of Lansdale, Pennsylvania — whose mother, father, sisters and brothers each follow God's plan to serve others by working together. They put into play a winning team spirit, enabling them to become outstanding teachers, coaches, and active community contributors. They have touched and continue to positively impact so many other lives to make a profound, lasting and positive impact on literally tens of thousands of young people across three generations.

Football Family is also a compelling recapitulation about how a multi-generation family has jubilantly shared triumph while remaining emotionally dependent on one another in the stark face of horrible tragedy.

Beautifully written by Ms. Bridget Algeo – the fifth oldest of Jim and Mary Margaret "Mickey" Algeo's nine children – *Football Family* is more than just a football story or an homage to the achievements of a legendary high school coach of the gridiron. It is an insightful celebration of a devout Catholic man who realized that God's plan for him was to serve others, not as a person of the cloth, but as a giving, loving individual who used other types of "pulpits"... in the classroom, on the gridiron, and in the community to make a significant difference in others' lives.

Coach Algeo's success is a tribute to the devotion he put forward in his students, his athletes, and his wife and children. He played a significant role to help them become successful within his realm, and after they transitioned into college students and adults.

As a sportswriter who covered Lansdale Catholic athletics from the fall of 1977 through the spring of 1981, I saw first-hand how Coach Algeo made a profound impact on his student-athletes.

Because his student-athletes were well-served and became successful, Jim Algeo, Sr. has earned and has been recognized with a multitude of impressive honors.

The same year his 2004 Lansdale Catholic Crusaders competed for the Pennsylvania state championship, he was inducted into the Pennsylvania Football Coaches Association Hall of Fame. Four years later, he was named the second-ever Robert T. Clark Award winner at the 71st Annual Maxwell Football Club's 2008 event.

A 2011 inductee into the National High School Athletic Coaches Association Hall of Fame in Grand Rapids, Michigan, Coach Algeo combined his passion for teaching and coaching with a father's love. He spent a lifetime serving as a staunch ally and demanding leader of young people, coaxing and enabling his students and athletes to succeed in all of their endeavors.

His 295 victories in 44 years as head football coach at Lansdale Catholic High School rank Coach Algeo among the top 20 coaches in the entire state of Pennsylvania.

What adds even more to this compelling "feel good story" is that Mickey and Jim instilled these same qualities in their nine sons and daughters, several of whom have gone on to become teachers and coaches. And, those who went into business or related callings are regarded as solid "teammates" in those fields. Each child has made a significant impact on others, in the classroom, on the sporting turf or arena, in the boardroom, and in the community.

Perhaps Bridget put it best when she reflected on her upbringing. "I was raised on the concept of team. Not only within my family, but with the young ladies who worked alongside me as student-athletes to achieve a common goal and strive for excellence while shooting for championships. Team comes in so many forms, like a classroom full of kids undertaking a service project."

Coach Algeo and his oldest child, Maggie Algeo deMarteleire, became the first father-daughter tandem to earn induction into the Montgomery County (Pennsylvania) Sports Hall of Fame. Following in her dad's footsteps, Mrs. deMarteleire built an impressive girls basketball program at North Penn High school in Lansdale. In her 15 seasons at the Lady Knights' helm, Coach deMarteleire led the Crusaders to 10 PAC-10 titles, 15 district playoff berths, and seven attempts for the state championship. She ended her coaching career with a whopping 534 wins registered by young lady athletes from both Lansdale Catholic and North Penn.

Jim Algeo, Sr. also had the privilege of coaching each of his sons; Jim, Jr., Dan, and John Patrick in addition to his grandson, Mike deMarteleire, Jr. He also has coached with all four, in addition to his son-in-law, Mike deMarteleire, Sr., as part of his LC football staff. Two of his sons have advanced to coach successfully at the varsity high school level. Jim Algeo, Jr. is an assistant coach at Spring-Ford High School following a similar and lengthy stint at Pottsgrove High School. Danny became one of only two head coaches to win Catholic League football titles with different schools – at Roman Catholic in 1999 and Cardinal O'Hara in 2004.

In addition, Jim, Jr. and Mary Wilson's daughter (Coach Algeo's granddaughter), Shannon Algeo, recently completed her third season as head women's lacrosse coach at Gwynedd Mercy University after a two-year stint as assistant coach at Marywood University in Northeastern Pennsylvania.

When speaking or writing about the Algeo family, you might say that the ball didn't fall too far from the (kicking) tee.

*

The "Rare Breed"

You will read the phrase "Rare Breed" throughout this story. According to the Merriam Webster Dictionary, a "rare breed" is "a relatively rare group". The website Rare Breed, LLC states that the concept of "Rare Breed" was born in 1968 in Lansdale, Pennsylvania. It is a phrase that signifies the toughness, determination, and commitment made by student-athletes and coaches involved with the Crusaders' football program.

I take that to mean that the group's members are special…they possess virtues and skills that are both specific to the task at hand, and which many others cannot and do not possess.

By its very nature, the sport of football requires a certain mental and physical toughness to play, and an undying commitment to try, try again when it comes to game-planning against opponents who may be bigger in size and numbers, and more talented at key positions.

For me, being a "rare breed" type of athlete at Lansdale Catholic High meant someone who one who would run through a brick wall to make a tackle, throw a block, or reach the end zone without a second thought.

And that's what I witnessed "back in the day."

As a sportswriter for *The Reporter* (previously named *The North Penn Reporter* until its sale to Gannett Corporation in 1980) in Lansdale, Pennsylvania, I saw first-hand the "Rare Breed" spirit of LC football in every student-athlete and coach, and on every down in every game. As one Intercounty League rival school's linemen put it following a tough loss to the Green and Gold, "Man, they just never quit. They play the game like every play is the most important one."

This "Rare Breed" spirit is the embodiment of the school's football program. It also reflects and represents the Algeo Football Family, and its members' commitment to serving God, serving the school and community, and serving their fellow man on and off the gridiron.

I am pleased to share the following special moments, both from my experience of covering LC's "Rare Breed" of football, as well as my treasured relationship with the Algeo Football Family.

*

A Relationship for the Gridiron.....and Beyond

It's somewhat ironic that as a print and broadcast journalist, I have been able to intelligently cover organized football at a high level. As we shall see, I have Jim Algeo, Sr. to thank for that.

You see, I never played the game. Despite my large frame en route to becoming a 6-foot-1, 260-pound adult, I never endured or completed a block or tackle during an organized football game.

Fearful of the potential for physical and even mental injury with which the gridiron would surely punish me, my mom, Marlene "Mickey" Alper Stern, refused to sign the parent permission slip allowing me to play football for the Olney Eagles and later, at Olney High School in Philadelphia.

Our dad, Ray Stern (of blessed memory), went along with Mom despite the fact that he was a huge college and pro football fan who spent many a weekend day watching games unfold on the family television.

I did play high school varsity baseball; I made up for my lack of speed with a lack of range. I was a good hit, but klutzy defensive player. I could've served as a designated hitter, but in the early 1970s, the DH wasn't yet a part of high school baseball. But I did become a first-rate in-uniform scorekeeper and play-by-play announcer of Olney High JV and varsity baseball.

Thankfully, God gave me the talent to write and speak clearly and with some creativity and sense of drama, enough so that my skill set eventually led me to the sidelines and press boxes of inner-city and suburban Philadelphia, Pennsylvania and Dallas, Texas. I became a reporter/writer, moving into the magical realm of the high school, college, and pro gridiron.

My God-given writing talent also led me into a fortuitous relationship with the Algeo family, one that has reinforced my tenets regarding faith and family.

As both a print and broadcast journalist, I have been blessed to cover football amid the color and excitement at various north Texas high school football venues under the lights, and at Cowboys Stadium in Arlington, Texas. I also have reported from the sidelines during college football games at Texas Christian University, Southern Methodist University and the University of North Texas, and on the professional level at cathedrals such as Veterans Stadium in Philadelphia and the Superdome in New Orleans, Louisiana.

Yes, I have experienced the buzz of speaking live on-camera amid the roaring crowds, reporting on a crucial victory or a demoralizing setback, and have felt the buzz associated with on and off camera interviews involving much-idolized coaches and players.

But the most lasting, meaningful and rewarding relationship I have ever enjoyed within football has been and still is with Lansdale Catholic High School Head Football Coach Jim Algeo, Sr. and his loving family. In addition to reinforcing my values of family and friendship, covering Coach Algeo and his LC "Rare Breed" student-athletes taught me more about football – and how it is played — than I ever could have hoped.

*

Hello, Coach Algeo

I joined *The North Penn Reporter*, a Monday through Saturday newspaper based in Lansdale, Pennsylvania in September of 1977. This was just a few months after I became the first member of my family to earn a college diploma, a Bachelor of Arts degree in Communications at Temple University in Philadelphia.

To say I was "green behind the ears" was an understatement. I was very knowledgeable about team sports and had traversed my share of football sidelines, basketball scorer's tables, and baseball backstops as a student-journalist at Olney High and at Temple's 90.1 megahertz radio station, WRTI-FM. I had written for newspapers and magazines and had broadcast play-by-play, color commentary and post-game recaps on radio.

But I had a lot to learn, and I knew it.

After spending the '77 football season covering Bux-Mont League schools in outlying communities such as Doylestown (CB East and CB West) Perkiomen Valley, Upper Perkiomen, Souderton, Ambler (Wissahickon) and Quakertown as a part-time writer, I had proven myself worthy of being hired full-time just as the basketball season was tipping off.

When I was assigned to the Lansdale Catholic High School athletics beat in December 1977, someone in *The North Penn Reporter* newsroom mentioned to me that Coach Algeo could be very loud and offensive, or words to that effect. When I entered the school for the first time, to cover my inaugural Crusader sporting event – a boys basketball game – the very first person to greet me was... Jim Algeo, Sr. He had the build of an interior lineman, with thick shoulders and arms...and a friendly Irish ear-to-ear grin. He shook my hand in earnest, thanked me for coming and for covering that night's game, and did so with a very soothing, reassuring voice. He also complimented me on my writing.

I suddenly realized that the description of Coach Algeo was from the practice field during the week, and from the sidelines on game day. To a young, unsure sportswriter, he was every bit the gentleman, educator, and ambassador.

Little did I know that this marked the onset of a lasting professional and personal relationship with Coach Algeo and his engaging, loving family. This friendship would enable me to understand what the Rare Breed commitment is, and the lessons and virtues of a Football Family.

*

The "Game Within the Game"

For me, a rookie sportswriter, Coach Algeo was an endless source of information that I used to add depth to my coverage of football, whether it was Lansdale Catholic, other high schools, or Coach Dick Vermeil's Philadelphia Eagles.

I was in relentless pursuit of information regarding the proverbial "game within the game," and would ask questions on the team bus to and from Intercounty League schools located in southeastern Pennsylvania towns like Robesonia, Birdsboro, and Reading, as well as after practices and games.

I also would speak with the coach when he attended other LC sports events such as girls and boys basketball and baseball. For example, this was how I learned about the importance of why an offensive lineman had to "explode" through their opponents on the defensive line while continuously pumping their feet. On the opposite side of the ball, I learned that the effective linebacker needed to take small steps in the direction of the read on the offensive linemen. And, upon making contact with the ball carrier, how and why the linebacker had to transition his arms from back to front in order to "wrap him up" and complete the tackle.

This lesson, and countless others related to the gridiron, helped make me a better writer and broadcaster when I relocated to football-religious Texas a few years later.

*

Drama on the Sideline

Contemporary facilities enable many of today's sports reporters to sit in some form of a press box where they keep ongoing statistics and make notes for use in their game stories. But in the fall of 1978 in Pennsylvania, journalists covering high school football dressed appropriately for the weather and traversed the sideline of the team they were covering with legal pad and writing implement(s) in hand. A good pair of sneakers was also an important tool of the trade.

With "tools" in hand (and on my feet), I was poised to document stats from the next play. Then the drama caught my eye. I watched it unfold on the Lansdale Catholic sideline just a few feet away during my inaugural experience of covering Crusaders' varsity football. It was a warm Indian summer evening at Pennbrook Middle School Stadium, and midway through the first quarter senior defensive lineman John Walsh and Head Coach Jim Algeo were discussing containment of the opponents' rushing attack in a somewhat animated tone.

Walsh said something along the lines of "Coach, I'm bangin' and hittin' 'em and I got my footing and they're sliding away from me and they're holdin' me and I'm this close from making the tackle." John had respectfully removed his helmet to address his mentor. He was yelping in the direction of his coach, in a very uncharacteristic mood, his face sweating profusely and his eyes wild with emotion, overexertion, and confusion.

Walsh, the latest in a steady line of brothers who studied and played football at LC, had blond hair and good looks that gave him a strong resemblance to actor Richard Thomas's portrayal of character John-Boy Walton in the TV show *The Waltons*. And he was definitely out of character. On the basketball court, classroom, and locker room, he was quiet, mannerly, and soft-spoken. Put him on a gridiron, and he quickly transformed into a Tasmanian devil.

Coach Algeo quickly responded to Walsh, marking the first time I would hear "The Voice." He bellowed something like "You gotta get in there and make a statement!"

Not unlike other gridiron gurus, the coach's gameday demeanor was somewhere between a union rabble-rouser on a strike line and an embattled general leading his troops onto a beachhead. Coach Algeo was growling in his trademark tenor as he gestured wildly with his clipboard and glared at Walsh. "We didn't practice this scheme and technique all week for them to go through us like a hot knife through butter! You gotta make a difference in there, John. They'll (his LC teammates) follow you anywhere, but you gotta lead the way. Now get back in there, make a tackle and make a difference!!!"

Although the player and coach seemed to be arguing with each other, they were actually verbally working through a disturbing issue that threatened to derail the Crusaders. Coach Algeo taught, game-planned and led his athletes with an uncompromising passion, and that trait (along with several other virtues) often rubbed off on his student-athletes to make them proficient players and better people.

Walsh and his defensive teammates altered their technique, began controlling the line, and enabled the offense to work its magic en route to a triumph. As the game continued, Coach Algeo amicably tapped Walsh's shoulder pad as the two discussed a specific approach to containing the opponent's attack. They also exchanged the kinds of glances that indicated they had worked through their issues, and that everything had returned to normal.

Interviewing Coach Algeo at midfield post game, I found him to be even-mannered and calm of voice, humble in victory, and extremely accommodating while answering my questions.

Later, while writing the game story at *The North Penn Reporter* offices at 307 Derstine Avenue, I reflected on the sideline conversation between the coach and John Walsh.

It confirmed what I initially realized — that Jim Algeo, Sr. was indeed a very special leader of students and athletes.

*

The "Growl" and A Fatherly Voice

During each autumn of the three seasons that I covered Lansdale Catholic football for *The Reporter*, I would visit one of their practices each week to speak with Coach Algeo and his student-athletes for feature stories and a preview of the upcoming opponent.

I always made sure to arrive early enough to watch the tail end of practice. This was a time when I might learn something with which to add some insights, some depth, to my coverage of football.

I also was able to watch the unfolding of another drama, one that reflects the ongoing rapport between the players and their coaches. In addition to the screaming and yelling that highlight each session, there were also those private chats between a coach and player.

Coach Algeo and his assistants managed to combine a sense of urgency with patience, an unbridled passion with a fatherly arm around the shoulder, and a gruff, intimidating growl with the soft voice of one-on-one teaching and understanding.

I was certainly amazed that Jim Algeo, Sr. could maintain his patience and remain in control while – at the same time – emoting with a strong passion for teaching and football as he yelped at a player struggling to perform a certain task. It provided me with a successful approach, one that helped me years later when I made the transition from the business world into teaching.

*

Veer Left

When the 1978 season began, Lansdale Catholic lost a tough 8-7 non-league verdict to nearby rival Souderton Area, then opened the Intercounty League season at home against Reading Central Catholic. Senior quarterback Jim Algeo, Jr., who did not play against Souderton, was behind center. In anticipation of covering Jim's first varsity start, I wrote the phrase "return of the warrior" in my advance article, which young Jim said, "gave me a lot of self-esteem, if not a big head."

By Jim's own admission, his play was "a series of fits and spurts," but he remained a true team leader with his confident body language and inherent leadership skills.

The game was scoreless at halftime, with both teams hungry for a victory that would provide momentum in what everyone anticipated would be a difficult trek through an ultra-competitive Intercounty League schedule. After the Cardinals drew first blood with a field goal, LC tailback Owen Collins erupted for a 50-yard run to put his team within striking distance of scoring.

Jim brought the offense – his offense – to the two-yard line to run a play called "Veer Left" against a tough Cardinal defense.

At the snap, Jim faked a handoff to burly fullback Tom Famularo, who slammed ahead into the interior defensive line in hopes of moving defenders backward and creating some space for his QB. At some point during my coverage of LC football, I assigned Tom the nickname "Fam the Ram" because he routinely drove tacklers backwards five yards upon contact with his strength, bulk and determination.

Moments later, QB Algeo quickly faked a pitchout to Collins, who was sprinting outside toward the left sideline to draw the defensive backs' attention. At some point during my coverage of LC football, I assigned Collins the nickname "Towin' Owen" because – in addition to his speed – he had the ability to carry tacklers a few extra yards.

With would-be tacklers converging on the only open spot along the goal line, QB Algeo safely tucked away the pigskin and burrowed his way into the end zone to give the Crusaders a 6-3 lead as the bleachers crammed with LC fans behind me erupted.

Moments after the 16-3 victory had ended, I asked Jim, Jr. how it felt to cross the goal line in such a small space, and at such a crucial point in the game. "You know," he said with a jubilant smile, "it was a simple read."

He continued to verbally outline the play, then turned quiet and intro-spective. He suddenly realized that my question had a deeper meaning. "It's football," he said. "That play is what football is all about. You work hard all week in practice as a closely-knit team, as a family, really. And you do your best to deliver when the moment of truth arrives."

Those comments helped introduce me to the "Rare Breed" climate, the team's cohesiveness, and its capable on-field leadership.

A few months later they would celebrate winning the 1978 Intercounty League championship.

*

Happy Halloween

En route to capturing that title, the Crusader defense used their game performances to put on weekly clinics on how to stifle an opponent's run and how to completely shut down a rival's passing attack. The D of LC was so effective, they allowed an unheard of average of just seven points per game.

Their defense was so solid and ferocious, a type of scary good unit that literally struck fear in the hearts of opposing offensive coordinators, that I decided to write a tongue-in-cheek piece in *The North Penn Reporter* to commemorate the approaching Halloween celebration.

The article highlighted both the unit's and various individuals' multitude of achievements and statistics, with a "suggestion" that readers could visit the Crusaders' locker room and borrow "fearsome" defensive players' uniforms that would impress their fellow Trick or Treat colleagues.

When I spoke with Coach Algeo later in the week after the article ran, he informed me that someone had actually visited the locker room to heed my suggestion.

*

Good One!!!

Coach Algeo was kind enough to allow me to ride the team bus when the Crusaders visited an Intercounty League rival's stadium in Berks County. Most of these games were played on Saturday afternoon, and since *The*

Reporter did not print a Sunday edition, I didn't have to rush back to the office to file my story. Instead, I was able to discuss football with the coaches and bond with the students whom I was covering.

This also enabled me to witness an emotive tradition spanning four decades – the head coach's official proclamation of a job well done to achieve victory.

Following a 39-0 road victory over Schuylkill Valley High early in the 1978 season in Leesport, Pennsylvania, I interviewed both coaches as well as several LC student-athletes on a sun-splashed Berks County afternoon. Then I boarded the bus right before Coach Algeo slowly climbed the three steps onto the front of the bus, his face a mask of joy, confusion, and disappointment. At one point, I thought he would tear into his team for not beating the opponent more soundly – they did not score a point in the second half.

Slowly, Coach Algeo turned toward his silent student-athletes, stared at them for a moment...then animatedly pumped his first in the air and bellowed "Good One!" as his face relaxed into a gratified smile. This elicited a roar of happiness from his teenage players as the bus driver released the brake to begin a satisfying trip home.

*

Happy Holidays

I am aware that journalists are expected to maintain a steadfast separation from those whom they write about. But sometimes, life gets in the way. Or perhaps, God has a different plan.

Such was the case during the Christmas season of 1978, when I received an invitation to spend Christmas Eve at the Algeo home on Columbia Avenue in Lansdale. In addition to showing their gratitude for my passionate writing about the student-athletes at Lansdale Catholic and throughout Bucks and Montgomery Counties, I believe that the family members had in some ways grown close to me – and vice-versa.

Our relationship had grown as I covered Mary Margaret Algeo's basketball games and quarterback Jim Algeo, Jr. on the gridiron. I would visit with Mickey and the younger children sitting in the bleachers and awaiting the teams' pre-game appearances. Those younger Algeo kiddoes would embrace me as if I were a long-time family acquaintance.

I would also chat with middle school student Danny Algeo, discussing everything from the Flyers and Eagles to other LC sports. Dan and I would talk as football fans and friends at LC football practices and games, and at other sporting and school events. It didn't matter that Dan had not yet entered high school and I was in my mid-20s – we could converse as equals.

Dan displayed a maturity far beyond his pre-teenage years. In fact, even before he attended LCHS, Dan exuded a significant degree of pride in LC's student-athletes, his dad Jim, Sr. as the head football coach, and his brother Jim, Jr. as the on-field leader – the quarterback. "Thanks for giving us so much great ink (i.e. newspaper coverage)," he said on numerous occasions in his enthusiastic lilt, always accompanied by the ear-to-ear grin that made him an absolute pleasure to visit with. "I love reading about the team, and I know they (student-athletes) do as well."

Needless to say, I was comfortable in the company of everyone in the Algeo family, and they enjoyed my presence. As a result, the Algeo family invited me to their home for Christmas Eve dinner, a practice that would be repeated in the near future for several occasions of celebration, including Easter Sunday.

Jim and Mickey, along with their eldest kids, were aware that I am of the Jewish faith, albeit one who to this very day enjoys the magic of holidays celebrated by other denominations.

On December 24, 1978, I joined the 11 members of their family. As we sat down to enjoy the occasion, a reassuring, peaceful quiet settled over the table. With everyone holding hands, Jim, Sr. recited a heartfelt prayer, after which each member of the family wished me and one another a Merry Christmas.

Just a few seconds had passed when the first course was being served. I suddenly realized that Jim, Jr. – who had skillfully led the Crusaders to the Intercounty League title as a senior quarterback – was looking across the table at me. He had a confused look on his face, then made his decision to audible. "Mike, Happy Hanukkah to you," he said in a voice much softer than the one he'd used at the line of scrimmage.

Just about everyone – myself included – laughed during this moment of wonderful inter-religious fellowship.

The comment underscored how Jim, Sr. and Mickey had taught their children to respect and engage people of different religious backgrounds, beliefs, and races.

It is also one of those endearing, loving moments forever etched in my head, and in my heart.

*

The Jacket

When I was 25 and still single, I moved from Lansdale to Fort Worth, Texas in September 1981 to become the media relations director of the Fort Worth Texans, a Central Hockey (i.e., Triple-A) affiliate of the Colorado Rockies (now the New Jersey Devils).

Thus, the Algeo family and the school did stay with me in the form of an inanimate object – a much-cherished heavy-duty white Lansdale Catholic jacket with "CRUSADERS" festooned in a circular pattern on the back, and the school's name in green lettering on the upper left-hand corner of the front.

The Algeos had given me the jacket as a Christmas gift the previous December. Although I kept it in the closet while still living in Hatfield, I proudly wore it in football-crazy north Texas when the weather turned cooler. The jacket also somehow attracted the attention of a player agent who thought I was a football player from the University of Georgia or the University of Texas when I arrived at the Loews Hotel in Dallas to cover the Cotton Bowl.

I continued to wear that jacket whenever I covered Dallas-area high school football for the *Dallas Morning News* and the now-defunct *Dallas Times Herald.* But I did not maintain contact with the Algeo clan in those pre-Internet years. Totally immersed in my career, I would soon meet my first wife, Ilene and start our family when she gave birth to our son, Jordan. Ilene also donned the jacket on occasion – what was mine was hers.

One evening when I was searching for it, my wife Ilene (of blessed memory) apologized to me – she had given the jacket away to a homeless person who was shivering on a street near the mall in Mesquite, a suburb of Dallas.

Although not thrilled with this turn of events, I quickly realized that the loving, giving spirit of the Algeo family – and by extension of the St. Stanislaus parish and Lansdale Catholic High – had reached across 1,600 miles on a chilly afternoon in north Texas to bless someone in need.

*

Reconnecting

Through Jim, Jr. and Dan, I happily reconnected with the Algeo family in 2012 when social media emerged as a new, effective form of communication. Despite the 31 intervening years and miles that still stood between us, Jim, Jr. Dan, Bridget and Ronni and I eagerly "friended" one another via Facebook. Thus, I began reliving and celebrating anew the multitude of wonderful memories…of my roaming the sidelines, writing stories, and enjoying their engaging company.

During a December 2013 trip to nearby Warrington to visit my parents, my wife Colleen and I accepted an invitation to have dinner and catch up at the home of Mary Margaret and Mike deMarteleire in Harleysville. As the evening unfolded, each of us realized that the years and miles in between had done nothing to alter our friendship. Colleen and I spoke of our children, their spouses and grandchildren. We bragged about my son Jordan Stern, a professional baseball player turned successful business executive in Frisco, Texas, and of Colleen's daughter, Heather Meek, an elementary school principal in Texas and son Shawn Higgins, a technical executive also in Texas.

This was a glorious evening during which Colleen met Coach and Mickey Algeo, along with Jim, Jr., his wife Mary and their daughter Shannon, Dan and his daughter Becca, and Mike deMarteleire, Jr.

Before we departed, Dan took me aside and told me he was sorry to hear that my first wife, Ilene, had passed away in June 2009. "I know you will never forget her," he said to me. "And I'm glad that you are living a fulfilled life in the aftermath of that tragedy."

*

Talking Up the Algeo Family on the Airwaves

Well before this outstanding work was written by Bridget Algeo, I had the pleasure of sharing some of the Algeo family's achievements as part of high school football and basketball broadcasts emanating in suburban Dallas and reaching the far corners of this nation and even the world.

During the Fall and Winter from 2015-2018, I provided play-by-play accounts of varsity high school events via streaming audio/video on the NFHS (National Federation of High School Associations), a high school sports media firm launched in 2006. Working the games with me as color analysts were emerging electronic and print student-journalists such as Nicole Stuessy, Johnny Hobart and Michelle Brooks of McKinney High (McKinney, Texas), Dylan Villa of McKinney North High (McKinney, Texas), and Nick Kucholtz and Austin Meek of Frisco Wakeland High (Frisco, Texas).

On air, I highlighted some of our between-action conversations by regaling the audience and these student-broadcasters with stories about the

Algeo family. If we were calling a football game, then I'd animatedly discuss the impact on student-athletes of Jim Algeo and his sons. And when we were calling action for basketball, I'd proudly share with our audience the outstanding achievements of Maggie Algeo deMarteleire and her North Penn Lady Knights.

I also shared the memory of those exciting Algeo family achievements with my broadcasting colleagues off-air, as well.

*

A Show of Respect and Love

When my dad, Ray Stern was in failing health in June 2017, I flew into Philly from Dallas to see him and "say goodbye". I also caught up with Jim, Sr. and Mickey Algeo, as well as two of their daughters, Bridget and Veronica.

My dad, a Korean War veteran, passed away a few weeks later just two months shy of his 90th birthday. To honor him, we held a memorial service with a military honor guard at Washington Crossing National Cemetery in Newtown, Pennsylvania. Thirty minutes before the ceremony began, Bridget and her parents emerged from an SUV to pay their respects.

I struggled to control my emotions at this show of respect and love. The Algeo family was there in my time of emotional need, and I was extremely proud to introduce the three of them to my mother, relatives, and close friends.

*

God's Plan

I was raised to believe in God. I was taught that He gives each of us the ability to be humble in success, to deal with failure or disappointment, and to rally to once again achieve some level of victory in the game of life. And as an adult, I have come to know, appreciate, and actually live what many refer to as "God's plan."

A few years ago, when I rejoiced at reconnecting with the Algeo family, I also hoped and prayed for the opportunity to again write about and/or broadcast their journey, and how they have impacted so many young lives.

The Lord's plan has called for me to fulfill that wish, via a request from author Bridget Algeo to set the table by writing the foreword for this outstanding work.

This journey has enabled me to joyfully and enthusiastically recall and write about some of the most memorable experiences that I have had in covering, reporting about and enjoying my professional and personal relationship with the Algeo family.

I sincerely hope and pray that you enjoy the Algeo family's compelling story as much as I have in introducing you, or reconnecting you with this loving, giving and wonderful *Football Family*.

Introduction

Dressed in the unusual attire of a tuxedo and sitting amidst some of the biggest names in collegiate and professional football, a quiet white-haired man casually chatted with the likes of Tim Tebow, Vince Papale, and Andy Reid at the 2008 Maxwell Football Club Awards in Atlantic City, New Jersey.

His wife, their nine grown children, their spouses, and all of his grandchildren were there as well. In spite of the affair being a six-hundred dollar a plate event and well beyond the budget of our small town Pennsylvania family, we *all* were there — gowns, tuxedos, black ties, and all.

Our family was seated among hundreds that evening, and we could feel an unforgettable buzz of excitement filling the air in anticipation of the awards ceremony. Tom Brady was to receive the Professional Player of the Year Award, with Bill Belichick being honored as its Coach of the Year. For the second year in a row, Tim Tebow had been named the organization's Collegiate Player of the Year.

For this Irish-American Catholic clan from Lansdale, Pennsylvania, this kind of event was like nothing we had ever attended.

For the prestigious Maxwell Football Club, it was old hat. For the 74th year in a row, it was gathering to honor football's finest at every level of the game. The club's long history has been lined with the sport's greatest names: Peyton Manning, Johnny Unitas, Paul Hornung, Terry Bradshaw, Joe Theismann, Dan Marino, Joe Montana, Brett Favre, and so many other legends who have etched their way into the hearts and memories of football fans everywhere.

In the meantime, Philadelphia sports legends Ron Jaworski, Harry Kalas, and others conversed with the small, unknown, white-haired man decked out in rare and rented formal attire. He was to accept one of the

Maxwell Club's newest honors, the Robert T. Clark Award for Outstanding Contributions to the Game of High School Football.

It was only the second time in the club's history that an award for high school football accomplishments was being given to a recipient other than a player. The year before, Central Bucks West Head Football Coach Mike Pettine earned the inaugural honor.

If you never heard of Coach Mike Pettine, Sr., you may have heard of Mike Pettine, Jr., an all-state quarterback who became the head coach of the Cleveland Browns in 2014. Currently the defensive coordinator for the Green Bay Packers, his roots reach back to a place just minutes from where we grew up. His father, the older Mike, was a legendary high school football coach from Bucks County, Pennsylvania. I knew the Pettine name by the time I was seven years old.

If you search for and watch *The Last Game*, an ESPN documentary, you will learn more about why and how Mike Pettine, Sr. left his mark on high school football — and why the Maxwell Club saw fit to honor him. Even popular media presence Mike Smerconish remembered his former coach in a tender farewell when he passed away suddenly at the age of 76 in February of 2017.

For now, it is enough to know that, in thirty-three seasons as the head coach of the Central Bucks West High School Bucks, Coach Mike Pettine, Sr., amassed a record of 326 wins, 42 losses, and 4 ties. At one point, his program saw a 55-game winning streak. He coached 16 unde-feated seasons and led his team to 4 state championships. In 2007, the Maxwell Football Club recognized him for his remarkable achievements as a high school football coach.

On this night, March 8, 2008, the award would go to another man who left his print on the canvas of Pennsylvania High School football. Just who was he and what did he do? What was his record? What were his titles and his numbers? What did he win?

He was my father. He won many things, but, most importantly, what he did was create what I would always know as our Football Family.

~ FAMILY ~

CHAPTER ONE

Sunrise

But Ruth said, "Do not urge me to leave you or turn
back from following you; for where you go, I will
go, and where you lodge, I will lodge. Your people
shall be my people, and your God, my God.".

~ Ruth 1:16

When you read this chapter, you won't read much about football. Even with all the memorable football stories I was blessed to witness over the years and want to share with you now, you might even forget you are reading a book about football. I hope you do.

As for myself, I didn't start off as much of a football fan. At all. Before the age of seven, I complained every time my mom crammed me, and my brothers and sisters into the family station wagon to go to a game — especially the far away ones. Ugh, not *again*. Didn't we just all watch a game last weekend?

As the fifth child of James Michael and Mary Margaret Algeo, I did not have any choice in the matter. Wherever they were going, I was going. All nine of us, we were *all* going.

Most of my childhood was like that — together. We went to many places as a family. Rarely do I recall ever truly being alone.

In fact, one of the very few places I was ever actually by myself throughout my childhood was, ironically, in our family home where eleven people lived. It was a modest duplex with a basement, an attic, a single bathroom, one powder room, a small but lively backyard, and a two-car garage. Best part of all, it was three stories high, and I often found myself in the last room you could possibly go to on the third floor.

Many times as a young child, my family was gathered downstairs in the living room watching sporting events or other programs throughout the year. At times, I would join them. Other times, I disappeared upstairs.

Often I was on the highest floor of the house at a small desk stuffed with copybooks, paper tablets, and drawing pads. Sometimes I drew pictures, sometimes I wrote stories and poems, and sometimes I did a little of both.

Many times, I watched movies.

My love for movies went way beyond casual. I have been intrigued by this kind of storytelling for as long as I can remember. From the time I was a child, I lay on my bed watching movies from almost every genre happily for hours at a time.

For me, I was and still am fascinated by the special way film tells a story. The characters, the setting, the camera angles, the music, the script, the lighting, the sound … all of it comes together seamlessly in a well-made film that draws us in and to another place and time. The best movies will have me thinking about them for days and making me happy to watch them again year after year.

I've watched all kinds. I can't sing, but I know almost every word of most Rodgers and Hammerstein musicals. I have seen nearly every Alfred Hitchcock movie. I have gone for everything from the epics, the classics, Shirley Temple, Clint Eastwood, and the late-night black and white ones many people never heard of.

And, either with family or alone in my room, I have probably seen almost every football movie ever made. Most of these I have viewed on the small screen. Very few times have I actually gone to a movie theatre to watch an American film about football.

The one time I did was in 1996. The movie was *Jerry Maguire.*

Some people don't really classify it as a football movie. For me, it's close enough. If you haven't seen it and you want to, you may want to pause reading for about two hours and so. It's a good movie with Tom Cruise and Renee Zellweger, some catchy tunes, an engaging story, and a very enjoyable breakout Oscar-winning performance by Cuba Gooding, Jr.

Early in the film, we are introduced to a young man who is a professional sports agent now disenchanted by what the job he once loved has become. No longer driven by strong emotional connections to real people, it is devoid of meaning. The singular objective of the company he helped build is sales. Numbers are the most important thing.

One night, as he prepares to write a mission statement instead of a hollow and empty memo, he has a breakthrough moment. Questioning just what success is and whether or not his company understands it, Jerry faces the truth about his life.

He writes a free-flowing mission statement that calls his colleagues to a critical moment of transformation. At first, he is unsure if he will actually ever deliver the document. As he writes, however, his enthusiasm builds, and he goes in the next day with the 25-page invitation challenging his organization to return to its roots of caring deeply for its clients — in this case, young men and women looking for agents to represent them as they move into the professional sports arena.

As Jerry goes out on a limb to rally his co-workers to leave this company and join him, he is first applauded. He quickly finds out, however, not everyone shares his enthusiasm or are willing to take that risk. Some of them clearly think he has downright lost his mind.

Things don't bode well for him from there.

When he asks which of his colleagues is coming with on a new incredible journey founded on people, relationships, and trust, it is followed by an awkward silence that befalls the corporate office. Embarrassed, he begins to walk out of the office with the company fish.

At that moment, one Dorothy Boyd stands and shouts, to her own amazement and that of her office mates, that she will go with him. The two leave the office unsure and unconfident of what lies ahead.

But they go anyway.

I often think of my parents as a young couple when I see that scene.

No, they did not meet in a corporate setting, as you will soon read. Hardly. Neither did they both storm off the floor of their jobs together. In reality, there are probably more differences than similarities between Big Jim and Mick compared to Jerry Maguire and Dorothy.

But like the two movie characters awkwardly departing everything they have known without a clear map of the road ahead, my parents also knew only a few certain things as they moved into the future together. But they knew about the important things. They knew for sure to trust in God. They knew for sure the worth and dignity of people. And they knew for sure that they both believed in family.

Almost any family's journey through life is captured in memories. These moments and milestones, if we are fortunate, are collected in photographs, videos, journals, newspaper clippings, and other tangibles that help us remember the people, places, and things we never want to forget.

It doesn't matter, though, if we catch that great shot or record in writing the special memories a family makes as we move through space and time. No matter what, all these things we keep in our hearts, where we remember better than any other device invented in our modern world.

Though I love to take pictures, save mementos, and write things down, it is from my *heart* that I share the story of what became to us our "Football Family."

It was not perfect and had its ups and downs, but just like his wary coworkers were invited by Jerry Maguire to take the chance and join him on a ride that would be well worth it, me, my family and others were given that same chance to be part of a journey that bonds us like family.

Whether we liked it or not, we were going. And go we did.

What my heart recalls from my earliest memories are car rides. I can't even begin to guess how many different cars my parents had over the years. I can only say that only one was a brand new set of wheels, though it was years before I was born. Dad said it was a Studebaker, and Mom said it was a Rambler. Whatever it was, we were in those cars more than a lot of the time.

In whatever family vehicle it may have been, we traveled to many different places. They were not expensive, exotic, or more than a few hours away from home. Some we were excited about, others we were not. For me, the ones I was not all too thrilled about as a very young child ultimately became the ones that I cherish to this day.

Our family vehicle did not stray too far from the Philadelphia region. Mainly, we traversed the eastern part of Pennsylvania to attend football games. If we went beyond our state's borders, it was to visit family in Delaware, New Jersey, Maryland, and Florida.

Getting in a car to drive anywhere with family back then was so different than it is today. There were no DVD players or multiple devices to entertain us and keep us quiet for the road trip. There were seat belts, but you only put them on if you were lucky enough to be in a spot with two belts to snap together. Most of the time, we all had to squeeze into what was usually a station wagon. Little ones crawled into the back, and bigger kids squished together in the seats.

For several years of my childhood, my parents, with such a hefty clan, would actually take roll before we set out. It was generally a humorous experience, my mom calling out each of our "numbers", which were respective to the place we each held in the family.

"Number 1?"

"Here."

"Number 2?"

"I'm on a coffee break."

"Number 3?"

"Here."

"Number 4?"

"I jumped out the window."

Then our dad would start the car. We were off.

Wherever we went, our rides were basically quiet. Our trips almost always consisted of at least nine bodies in a modest vehicle, but it was rarely noisy. Sometimes the younger ones would cry or tell on each other, and other times the older ones would elbow one another in a low-key battle for territory across the imaginary lines in the crowded back seat.

Once we got rolling, the quiet would sometimes be broken by one of us requesting Dad to turn on the radio. To this day, it is why we know the words to many oldies tunes from the fifties and sixties. As a whole, we were not a musical family, but, in Irish-American tradition, we were raised on song. We would either be listening to 560 AM oldies or doing our best to recreate Rodgers and Hammerstein musicals. The complete rendition of *The Sound of Music* was arguably our "best" act.

If we weren't singing or playing games, I would generally, having positioned myself near the door, be looking out the window. When I got my license and began to drive years later, my family was astounded that I did not know the directions to places we had been easily hundreds of times.

"What were you doing?" they would ask incredulously.

"I was thinking about things," was my usual reply.

More accurately, I was dreaming. Had I said that, though, I would have been collectively ridiculed without hesitation. So "thinking" seemed like a safe choice of words.

"Thinking about *what*?"

Now when you are a dreamer, there is no way to fully explain what is going on in your head. I could write a whole separate book about everything I thought about as I gazed out the window on those long rides, and I would still never give all those ideas and scenarios dancing around my brain justice.

Nonetheless, my family remained astonished that I did not know how to get to my grandparents' house in Sharon Hill, Delaware County. It was a mere hour away, along a route that we had traveled to celebrate with our big old Irish family almost every weekend of my childhood.

My own logic was that I would learn it when I needed to know it, which I did. Why would I waste valuable car time studying directions when I could be looking into the clouds dreaming some of the best stuff ever?

While I was daydreaming into the clouds, my parents were taking us all over the Delaware Valley to different places. Three of them became very deeply special to our family. One of these three was to be alongside the ocean.

*

Beginning when we were in college, it was usual for my best friend Laura to share all kinds of items of interest she would come across in her research or homework. We would be studying quietly in our room when she would suddenly break the silence with, "Listen to this." She would then start reading aloud whatever she had found. The topic could be related to mathematics, logic, religion, philosophy, or nature, such as the ocean.

One night, she read a quote from President John F. Kennedy as he addressed America's Cup Crews in September of 1962. We were both mesmerized by the profound truth in his words as he spoke about the sea — not only the science of it, but the appreciation, connection, and deep attachment so many of us have to it:

"I really don't know why it is that all of us are so committed to the sea," spoke the thirty-fifth President of the United States, "except I think it's because, in addition to the fact that the sea changes, and the light changes, and ships change, it's because we all came from the sea. And it is an interesting biological fact that all of us have, in our veins the exact same percentage of salt in our blood that exists in the ocean, and, therefore, we have salt in our blood, in our sweat, in our tears. We are tied to the ocean. And when we go back to the sea — whether it is to sail or to watch it — we are going back from whence we came."

Over the years, I may have forgotten some of the things she read to me, but not Kennedy's sentiments about the earth's salt water. They expressed our strong bond with the ocean, something that resonates with many people. It always has with my family.

In fact, if you live in the Philadelphia suburbs, heading to the Jersey Beaches is known as going "down the shore". It is a summer tradition I have enjoyed since the earliest times in my life, way before I ever saw a football. These images are disconnected but vivid, but I had to be two or three years of age. I remember being afraid of the water and running away from it... being surrounded by not just my own family, but my many aunts, uncles, and cousins...all of us walking as a sort of chain gang to the beach by day and to the boardwalk rides by night.

Not being allowed to enter the rental after a long, sandy day at the beach was a ritual we all learned and practiced over the years. To this day, the scent of the green and white soap our families used takes me back to a metal tub filled with warm water outside the back door of the shore house I first remember as a child. Sometimes, I would be sitting in it with a sibling or cousin getting the sand washed off my skin and out of my hair by one of the grown-ups with that bar of soap.

Afterward, as the sun started to set and bedtime was nearing, I couldn't understand why our bathtub had become filled with ice and cans of beer. As time passed and I grew older, I discovered that, of the many things our Irish Catholic clan knew how to do, one was to celebrate well.

Wherever we gathered, our family celebrations were big and festive and filled with food, music, dancing, and wall-to-wall, room-to-room people. As kids, we played outside until dark before we came in for the evening fun.

It seemed no matter whose household we drove to, there was a long table that was at the center of the party. It was filled with all kinds of meats and rolls, cake, scones, and bottles of beer and glasses with ice and funny-smelling drinks. My parents and grandparents and aunts and uncles and their friends were all seated around it.

At one end was our Uncle Mike. Everywhere he went, he would travel with his guitar. He still does to this day. There would always come a point in the evening when he would open his case and start strumming his strings, and that was the cue for me, my brothers and sisters, and my cousins to gather around and fill in the spaces between the adults at the table.

My Uncle Dan would often be at Michael's side. If Mike was the musical lead for the evening, Daniel was the emcee. He would spontaneously and humorously quip throughout the night, causing roars of laughter among the grownups. The children laughed aloud as well, though rarely understanding why we were laughing along with the adults.

Near Uncle Mike would be my aunts — Eileen, Mary, Sally, and Bonnie — along with one of my cousins, Mary Kathleen. Together, they would provide back up to Michael's lead vocals as they delivered a joyous concert of all kinds of songs from Irish ballads to hymns to the modern-day country, folk, and rock classics. Even an original family tune called "Over The Hill" became part of our family tradition and remains to this day.

My mom and dad were not really part of the band, although sometimes my mom's voice could be heard above the mix of elderly, adults, teens, children and babies. My dad, like my Pop-pop, his father, who was usually seated beside him, sat at the end of the table, quietly singing along.

The only song he led was called the traditional folk song, "The Moonshiner". His voice was not the greatest, and, as he sang, he would change octaves, sometimes high, sometimes low, and sometimes cracking. "I'm a rambler, I'm a gambler, I'm a long way from home…"

We children sang along when we knew the words. If not, we were happy to let the adults do their thing as they rocked back and forth between funny, hearty ballads like "When Irish Eyes Are Smiling" and soft, sweet sometimes sad ones like "Danny Boy". Otherwise, we were content to sing what words we knew while waiting for our personal favorites: "Thank God I'm A Country Boy", "Grandma's Feather Bed", and "Johnny B. Good." When Michael sang them, we enthusiastically joined in loudly and often took to the living room rug to dance.

Now we could sing and dance all night — and sometimes we came close. But, no matter what, we knew the day's festivities were drawing to a close when we heard three songs: "This Old Guitar", "Let There Be Peace on Earth", and "God Bless America." Even as a child, it struck me that these closing songs were sung with great passion and heart.

Swaying back and forth, and sometimes even holding hands, the grown-ups would sing about our country with a genuine love. I am not sure I understood it at the time, but in looking back, it seems to me that they truly treasured my grandparents' decision to cross the Atlantic Ocean from Ireland to America.

And so our family's love affair with the ocean began.

In the early years, Mom and Dad took us to Northern Wildwood. At the end of my first-grade year, however, my parents announced they were taking us somewhere new. Sea Isle City. They had simply found a place considerably less expensive to rent.

Like a lot of things new or different, when we change from one thing to another, there's often resistance. A week before school let out in June of 1974, my mother announced that we were spending two weeks in Sea Isle, not Wildwood, and I couldn't understand why.

But that one simple decision proved to be a game-changer that produced years of special memories for our very big family.

The ride to Sea Isle from our hometown generally took three to four hours, but not because it was actually that far away. It's just that we got caught in the heavy traffic that continues to mark summer weekends to the Jersey shoreline from Atlantic City to Cape May. As we grew older, we realized that the trip, if timed right, was just about an hour and a half away. Brother Dan would always tell us to get over the Walt Whitman Bridge by seven in the morning, and we'd be fine.

Well, considering that Mom and Dad (mostly Mom) spent all morning packing the car, which didn't set out until near noon, we were lucky enough to get there by dinner time. "There" was a tiny pink house on one of Sea Isle's three main roads that run alongside each other between the ocean and the bay. It was a one-floor house about two and a half blocks from the beach. We thought of it as our summer home, but it was truly owned by an acquaintance who rented it to us at an affordable rate for our big Irish families.

The place had a kitchen, one bathroom, no television, and three bedrooms. We loved it. I never slept in a bed there until I was nearly twenty years old, and that was more than okay. Even as a college student, my cousin and I found ourselves laying down beach towels as "beds" on the kitchen floor one night because there was no space left, not even the bathtub or the cars. We didn't care. We just all enjoyed being together.

This "the more, the merrier" spirit came from my grandmother, Sarah Algeo. We lovingly called her Nanny. Her house was full to the brim on many occasions, and I never heard her or Pop-pop ever complain about not having enough of this or that to feed additional guests or put a beverage in their hand. We learned very early on the journey that what we had was enough, and we were happy to share whatever we had.

What we had was a big giant extended family that would come together in a small pink house every summer for the time of our lives.

One of my favorite memories was the summer of 1976. A few of my siblings had spent the week with my Nanny and Pop-pop after a huge party, with the understanding that they and my Aunt Eileen would get us to the pink house at the end of the week. I had just finished third grade, and, with the entire country celebrating our Bicentennial birthday and the summer Olympics of Nadia Comaneci, I was dreaming up a storm on that ride.

And, with the arrival of Hurricane Bell, a storm came into town in early August. It was heading straight to Sea Isle City just as we were. My grandparents and aunt packed us in a blue maverick and headed out from Chester County, right outside of Philadelphia, to reunite us with our parents.

I was 9 years old and will always remember the sight as we were approaching Sea Isle City. It was raining lightly as we headed toward the toll booth that preceded the bridge leading into town. I would say I saw a hundred cars, maybe more, heading our way. They were all leaving the beach haven, and we were the single car going into it.

We were greeted by a man at the booth who was head-to-toe yellow. He told my aunt that we were not allowed to enter Sea Isle. The entire island was being evacuated because of the hurricane, which was racing up the East coast and was due to hit hard overnight. With a quizzical look on his face, he peered into the small car.

"It was packed to the roof and three children were sitting on towels and sheets in the back seat," recalled Aunt Eileen vividly. "So when I told the officer that we needed to pick up a couple of children, he looked in the car and asked where were we going to put them."

There was a calm exchange between them for a few minutes. To this day, I am not sure exactly what she said to the man to let us through the toll booth, and, by the look on his face, I am not sure he did either. She did convince him she was "good at making space", and, within moments, we were silently heading over the bridge to Sea Isle and on the way to the pink house.

Now to be the lone car crossing that bridge on one side while everybody else was on the other side in a line of cars as far as we could see was more than a little unsettling. We all became silent as we were moving toward something scary and unknown. None of us had ever driven into a hurricane before.

Back then, there were no cell phones or technological ways to communicate with each other while traveling, except for stopping at a pay phone booth on the side of the road. If we saw one, none of us were getting out to use it, so we kept traveling toward our destination as the rain fell increasingly harder.

It was probably only fifteen minutes of riding in my aunt's Maverick from the bridge to the house, but it felt like hours. We worried about all of our other family members. How close were they? Were they coming? Would anyone even be at the house? Would we get out of Sea Isle in time? Where would we even go?

We were all so relieved when we finally pulled up to that little pink house. I dashed out of the vehicle, up the three cement steps, and swung open the screen door to the kitchen. I expected to find the house in a panic, everybody packing up and getting ready to evacuate like everyone else in Sea Isle.

Not at all. It was the typical Algeo family party sight, with everyone sitting around a table full of rolls, lunch meat, crackers, cheeses, punch, and all kinds of food and drink. The only thing missing was the music, but not a single aunt, uncle, or cousin in that kitchen showed a shred of concern that a major hurricane was pummeling the coast and on its way up to Cape May County.

My parents and the rest of my siblings came about an hour later, and, once all the clans arrived, we loaded up the party into six different vehicles in search of an evacuation center as the rain teemed down. The first place, a local high school gymnasium, was completely full, so we drove on. All the kids waited in the cars as we pulled into the American Legion parking lot to see if there was room for our huge family. When we got the okay signal from the grownups, we each grabbed a bag or two and ran through the rain into the building.

The hall was filled with people setting up camp along the outside of the giant room with army green cots. In the middle were tables to place our things. In the corner was a kitchen with a woman giving out sandwiches, juice, and bubble gum. Surrounding us were long giant windows that stretched all the way to the ceiling. I would later watch the rain beat against them as I fell asleep in the early morning hours.

But not before an Algeo party.

With it growing darker, the winds picking up, the rain pounding the roof, and a restlessness rising in the hall, there was only one thing to do. Out came Uncle Mike's guitar. One of the men in charge grabbed the microphone and directed people over to his corner, where a crowd gathered, and we all joined in song and dance for an hour or two before retiring to our cots.

Our clan had managed to turn even a natural disaster into a family celebration.

We returned safe and sound to our pink house the next day to three feet of water in the streets. It quickly disappeared and our summer fun down the shore went back to our usual traditions of all-day beach-going, amusement parks, late night card games, and paddle board tournaments in the driveway.

Our time at Sea Isle year after was a delight to the senses. The smells and sounds and sights never go away over time. I never wanted to leave, and I was always a little melancholy that last day. As I reached my teens, I had established my own personal tradition, as many of us did, of seeing the sunrise over the ocean one more time before cleaning the pink house and cramming into the car to go back to Lansdale.

Sometimes I would even tear up a little, knowing that likely fifty weeks would have to pass before I would be standing on the beach watching the sun bounce up over the waters again. I knew, however, we would be back because something deep always drew us here to leave family memories along the edge of the ocean that our grandparents had bravely crossed in their youth.

With our two weeks of nothing but family at the shore now over, the sunrise, like always, did not signify the end. It was the beginning. In fact, as more summers passed, I began to see that the vacation fell on the same two weeks of the calendar every year.

The dawn of the last day at Sea Isle, with the sun's rays glistening on the waters I would not see again until next year, meant two things. For one, we were going back to a bigger family. I came to understand over time that, once we returned, we shared our parents with about fifty boys every fall.

And, two? The last sunrise of an August morning along the shoreline of New Jersey was the start of high school football season in Pennsylvania.

CHAPTER TWO

Dreams in the Heart

That the LORD called Samuel;
and he said, "Here I am."

~ *1 Samuel 3:4*

A young man, a decision, a priest to help him hear his calling...a dream in the heart.

Perhaps one of the most renowned names in football is that of Notre Dame Football legend Knute Rockne, who coached the Fighting Irish from 1918 to 1930. There are two movies that I have seen that share his story. One is included in *Wake Up The Echoes*, a documentary telling the story of Notre Dame University and its historic love affair with football. The other is a 1940 film called *Knute Rockne All-American*, which depicts Coach Rockne's life from a young child until his tragic death.

The career numbers posted by Knute Rockne across 13 seasons were incredible. 105 wins, 12 losses, 5 ties. 6 National Championships. 5 undefeated seasons. An 88.1 percent winning rate.

More than the statistics, however, the legacy Rockne left at the beloved university standing in South Bend, Indiana was one of spirit and passion. Known for his close personal connection with his players, his love of team, and an uncanny ability to motivate young men, Knute Rockne remains one the most celebrated and respected coaches anywhere of all time.

Born in Norway on March 4, 1888, Knut Larson Rockne came with his family across the Atlantic Ocean when he was five years old, settling in Chicago, Illinois. He learned to play football in the streets of the Windy City, becoming a member of the local team, as well as earning a spot on the North West Division High School squad.

Upon graduation, Knute did not attend college right away. Instead, he worked at the Post Office, where he saved money for four years so that he could study his favorite subject of chemistry and become a pharmacist. At 22 years of age, he boarded a train to the University of Notre Dame.

One of the requirements of students at the institution was to participate in one of its sports programs. Though he was small, his great love for the sport of football made the decision easy for the talented athlete. In 1910, he was cut from the team due to being "undersized."

The rejection brought out Knute's large competitive nature, and, not only did he make the team the next season, but he transformed it by being part of the wildly successful forward pass, being named All-American, and going undefeated in his career with 22 wins, 2 ties, and 0 losses.

Following his senior year and graduation, Knute became an assistant in the chemistry lab, as well as an assistant football coach in 1914. When Head Coach Jesse Harper resigned three years later, Rockne was offered the position and faced with a major decision, as accepting it meant forgoing his career as a chemistry professor, for which he had studied and prepared for years.

As shown in *All-American*, Knute consults Father John Callahan as he ponders the move to make coaching his life's work. When he asks the good priest if he thinks he is making one giant error in judgment, Father Callahan assures the young man that it is never wrong to follow one's heart.

A young man, a decision, a priest to help him hear his calling...a dream in the heart. And for Knute, the next thirteen years would be the stuff of dreams, as, led by the small but stout "Swede", Notre Dame football established itself as one of the nation's most loved and respected collegiate sports programs of all time.

So beloved was Notre Dame Football that, in the spring of 1931, a third movie about it, though I've never seen it, was being made. Featuring a few of the Fighting Irish, including Adam Walsh, who once declared he would cut his throat for Rockne, and the renowned Four Horseman, *The Spirit of Notre Dame* asked Coach Rockne to be a technical advisor to the project.

On March 31, 1931, on a date I know well because the month and day would later become my birthday, "The Rock" tragically died as the plane on which he was a passenger could not make its way to Hollywood through the turbulent stormy skies. An admiring nation was left stunned and the Fighting Irish family heartbroken.

Ten years later, Warner Brothers immortalized Knute Rockne in a classic movie starring Pat O'Brien, who characterized Rockne's spirit and charm to near perfection, and Ronald Reagan, a young actor who would later become President of the United States. As a result of his being cast in the role of the legendary George Gipp, President Reagan affectionately became known as "The Gipper." In 1997, the movie, *Knute Rockne All-American,* was recognized by the United States Library of Congress and selected for preservation in their National Film Registry.

*

About the same time that the making of the movie *Knute Rockne All-American* was in the works, James Michael Algeo was born to Daniel and Sarah Algeo on September 2, 1936. Three years later, on May 26, 1939, Mary Margaret Filliben was born to John and Elizabeth Filliben.

By the release of Knute's biography in 1940, the Great Depression was coming to an end. Besides *Rockne's* picture, other big films embraced by the American public were *Rebecca, A Philadelphia Story,* and *Pinocchio,* which spun a top-five single by Cliff Edwards. Most of us know it as the Disney classic, "When You Wish Upon A Star." It joined popular songs by Artie Shaw, Glenn Miller, and Bing Crosby as favorites of the day.

Around the world, Benito Mussolini pulled Italy into Hitler's attack on France and Britain, Winston Churchill became Prime Minister of England, and Nazi Germany began its relentless 57-day bombing blitz on London.

At home across the Atlantic Ocean, an average new house cost $6,550, a gallon of milk 34 cents, bread was 8 cents a loaf, gas 11 cents per gallon, a single US postage stamp could be bought for a mere 3 cents, and it would be almost 20 years before my father, Jim, and my mother, Mary Margaret, would meet for the first time on my grandparents' front steps.

In the meantime, throughout the forties and most of the fifties, each of them would be figuring out what exactly was in their hearts to follow.

My mom, born Mary Margaret, was known as "Mickey" for most of her life. She was the only girl in a family of eight, and her father doted on the fair-haired daughter with her loose blonde curls and affectionate personality.

Though I never met him, I was told John Filliben had "a good dose of Irish in him", and my Nanny, Elizabeth, always believed this to be the root of his occasional temper flare-up. Around Mickey, however, he was calm and caring, and my Pop-pop would frequently sit her on his lap as he listened to every minute of the Philadelphia Phillies on the house radio many an easy summer afternoon in Glenolden, Pennsylvania.

As warm as she was with very young children, Elizabeth Filliben was otherwise stoic and blunt, and she didn't mince words with anyone past the age of seven. She was very involved in her children's lives, and, if she thought anyone crossed them, she made her presence known.

As my Pop-pop Filliben was a huge sports fan, my uncles played baseball and basketball, as well as swimming and diving. When Nanny saw that one of her sons was not getting the playing time she thought he deserved, she went straight to his coach to confront him. The exchange ended with her telling him that "he didn't know anything about coaching." Of course, his name was Dr. Jack Ramsey, who went on to coach the Seventy Sixers, the Braves, the Pacers, and the Blazers, with whom he won an NBA World Championship Title and earned himself a spot in the Naismith Memorial Basketball Hall of Fame.

As much as she enjoyed sports, too, and played with her brothers in the yard and along the street of their big Elmwood Street property, Mom did not have a flourishing sports career. She tried out for basketball, but was promptly cut because she shot the ball from a position that wasn't allowed in old school "girls basketball". Mickey didn't know there was a different set of rules for girls.

Being cut from the team didn't faze her. Mom went on to have a happy childhood at Saint Gabriel's Grade School and "Fabulous Fifties" teenage years at Notre Dame Academy. She learned the piano and the clarinet, sang in glee club, practiced art, was involved in theatre, had a thriving social life, and became Student Council Vice President — winning every vote in the senior year election except her own.

As graduation neared, there was a brief discussion with my Nana and Pop-pop on the direction Mickey's life would go after receiving her diploma. She did not feel pressure or an expectation to attend college, and, had she, Mom would have chosen nursing as a career. Her heart told her, however, to be a wife and mother.

She had been going steady with a handsome young man named Jack for three years, and things appeared to be on track upon graduation. Most of Mom's friends and family thought she would marry Jack and begin a family of her own with him.

Instead, Mickey and Jack parted ways, and she took a job at Maryknoll Fathers that summer. As one of four secretaries, Mom performed clerical duties for the Philadelphia branch, which sent missionaries overseas.

Her future, however, was nowhere near a continent away. Most of her life, just over a ten-minute drive away that consisted of a few simple turns and a ride down MacDade Boulevard, lived a young man who was growing up three years ahead of her. He was the oldest son of six children who spent much of his childhood with his head buried in *Catholic Boy* magazine. His name was James Michael Algeo.

When James was a third grader living on Reese Street in Sharon Hill, Delaware County, Holy Spirit Grade School sent home a subscription for young boys printed by the Holy Cross Fathers at Ave Maria Press of the University of Notre Dame. Every month, he waited for *Catholic Boy* to arrive at my grandparents' doorsteps so that he could read his favorite comic strip about the Saint Polycarp High School Boys Football team.

For the first time, he saw the game of football, which he mostly played among childhood friends on the recess yard at school or in the streets in front of their homes, in a different light. The kids on St. Polycarp's team had problems off the football field, and there to help them work through them all was their head coach. As Jimmy read story after story, his heart told him that being a coach and teacher like that character was something he wanted very much to do.

Year after year passed as Dad moved from a young boy toward childhood. The Reese Street clan would grow to six — three boys and three girls — and their family life became a mix of going to church, love of sports, lively dinner debates and conversations, and annual summer vacations "down the shore". And just as sand can little by little bury a thing, young Jim's dream of becoming a teacher and coach became covered by the layers of life as he navigated through his early teen years.

In many Irish-Catholic families in particular at the time, there was a strong expectation for one of the sons to become a priest. Dad will always say that Nanny and Pop-pop never told him directly they expected him to enter the seminary, but he felt the unspoken pressure just the same. The very same Holy Cross Fathers who sent him *Catholic Boy* magazines beginning when he was eight-years-old opened their doors to him in the late summer of 1951 some 693 miles away from home. He was fifteen.

For three years, Jimmy enjoyed life in South Bend, Indiana, only a mile from Notre Dame and Knute Rockne's legacy, where he enrolled in a preparatory seminary under the spiritual direction of Fr. Frank Gartland, who was at one time the editor of *Catholic Boy*. By August 1954, he was on track to enter Sacred Heart Novitiate in Jordan, Minnesota, where he was to study, in silence, for a year.

As soon as Jim arrived in Jordan, an isolated city that was only one-hundred years old with nothing in sight but an occasional train, he was immersed in prayer, chants, Latin, and indoor and outdoor labor. During the very first week, he was sent to a field with another seminarian, and they were given instructions to dig a hole. They were forbidden from speaking to each other as they shoveled in the middle of the field.

At three o'clock in the afternoon sharp, the church bell rang. For a few brief moments, the young men were to stop their work and, during one of the few times they were permitted to speak, pray aloud.

"O Sacred Heart of Jesus," began his field companion.

Startled, Jimmy turned to him, dropping his shovel. "Huh?"

He hadn't even heard the bell. Dad then realized that he was standing in the wrong field. It was not the field he had always dreamed about, and, even though he felt a pang of guilt for the expenses that his hard-working parents of six had invested in his seminary experience, he filled up the hole he had dug and made an appointment to see Fr. William Craddick, the Master of the Novitiate.

"All I want to do is teach and coach football," he told the priest that evening. Just like at Notre Dame, where Father Callahan told Knute Rockne to follow his heart, Father Craddick told Jim Algeo, just a few days shy of his eighteenth birthday, the very same:

"Then you must teach and coach football."

A young man, a decision, a priest to help him hear his calling...a dream in the heart.

And now a phone call.

It wasn't easy, but Dad called back home that night to tell Nanny and Pop-pop that arrangements had been made to travel home the following Monday. He wasn't there to see, as my Aunt Sally would describe later, his father hang up the phone and quietly cry in the backyard of their home. His father Daniel didn't say another word about it and, come Monday, picked Jimmy up at the North Philadelphia train station. They marched his belongings to the car, and, as Pop-pop closed the trunk, he turned to Jimmy.

"Jim," he said in his thick Irish brogue. "Now they'll be girls."

*

Mickey Filliben enjoyed working for Maryknoll Fathers and had formed fast friendships with two of her fellow secretaries, Theresa Blaney and Sally Algeo. The trio would often get together after work, going to parties, movies, and dining out.

Jim Algeo had left the study of the priesthood and, driven by a desire to play and learn football at a small college where he would get playing time, entered nearby Pennsylvania Military College just months later.

On August 2, 1957, *The Day Christ Died* by Jim Bishop topped the bestselling books, America was listening to Elvis Presley's "Teddy Bear", and James Algeo was stopping by his home on Reese Street after ROTC at Fort Meade.

Sitting on the front steps of his family's home was Mickey, alongside his sister Sally and their friend Therese, all preparing to go out on a Friday night. To this day, Dad remembers his first thought upon setting eyes on the slender, dark-haired, fair-skinned eighteen-year-old beauty:

"Hubba, hubba, ding ding ...," he sang to himself at the sight of her.

Mom vividly recalls being immediately mesmerized by the cadet's long lashes and dark curly hair. The two, however, wouldn't go on their first date until four months later, when Jim asked Mickey to attend his Senior Formal at PMC in December.

Within five months of the dance, the Pennsylvania Military College senior and the first year high school graduate began going steady on April 28, 1958 (they remember all their special dates without hesitation) and, later that summer, Jim decided to approach Mickey's parents on the subject of asking for her hand in marriage.

On a hot summer evening in 1958, John Filliben sat listening to the Philadelphia Phillies on the radio in his kitchen. At the small table across from him sat his wife, Elizabeth, and a stout fair-faced young man with a smattering of freckles, thick dark hair, and bright eyes that had won over their daughter.

"John," asked Elizabeth, "did you hear what he just said?"

It was hard for my grandfather to intently follow the Phillies' game and discuss my young father's intention to marry my mother at the same time. In the next room, quite able to hear the entire conversation was Mickey, who quietly laughed to herself as the awkward exchange moved through questions, explanations, and interruptions by the radio announcer as he shouted out the plays of the game.

After almost an hour, Mickey was called in to join them.

It was her turn to answer a few questions her parents — mainly Nana — had for her.

"You know he's Irish?" asked Elizabeth.

To Nana, that meant her son-in-law would no doubt have a temper just like the one her husband had a tendency to show. But to Mickey, marrying this Irishman meant something completely different. It meant being with a man who was driven and who came from a spirited family that sang, danced, laughed, and prayed together.

Perhaps more than any of those things, however, Mickey loved Jimmy's faith in God, his strong convictions, and his full knowledge of exactly what he wanted to do with his life. She didn't have to worry that he would give her whatever she asked for, as Jim wasn't quick to let her have her way just because she could. This quality was one she recognized and admired from the start. She knew he would make good, honest decisions and trusted him.

After Midnight Mass on December 25, 1958, a year after their first dance, Jim gave Mickey a ring.

"I want to teach and coach," he told her. "And I'm not going to make a lot of money. I want you to be my wife."

Mickey was tearful but smiling as she accepted the ring. "It's such a good deal, I can't turn it down."

And so the wedding date was set for May 2, 1959. Or so they thought. Another meeting was called, and this time it was between both sets of the couple's parents. It appeared they had concerns about the financial situation of the young pair and did not think they had banked enough money to get married and start a family.

Jimmy and Mickey, eager to be together and begin life's journey with each other, could have resisted the request of their parents to delay the wedding so that they could build up their savings. But, which was clear to me my entire life, my parents held their own parents in the highest regard and with the greatest respect. They honored their wish and married on October 17, 1959. They were not any richer than six months before. At least, not financially.

Heading into that summer, in an effort to swell up his monetary resources before the nuptials, Jim delayed his plans to find a teaching and coaching position. Instead, he took a fast position with a financing firm in Philadelphia. It wasn't his heart, but it was a job.

One day, as he was out collecting for the company, he passed by West Catholic High School for Boys. There on the field was the football team, dripping with sweat from the summer camp drills, just days before school was to begin. Jim parked the car. For the next hour, he stood on the field and watched in silence. It was everything he loved. The strategizing, the play calling, the strength, the speed, the power all wrapped up in one game with all types of boys battling for an odd-shaped ball covered in pigskin on grass.

Like the seventeen-year-old who had made a decision to leave the seminary as he stood in silence in the middle of a Minnesota field, Dad swiftly left the practice, called my mom from a pay phone, and drove straight to the Archdiocese of Philadelphia Office of Education. There, he applied to be a teacher and coach, now only days from September, hopefully in time for the upcoming school year.

A young man, a decision, a woman to help him hear his calling...a dream in the heart.

CHAPTER THREE

Three Green Fields

"These things I have spoken to you, so that in Me you
may have peace. In the world you have tribulation,
but take courage; I have overcome the world."

~ John 16:33

In a lifetime of watching movies, among them almost every football movie ever made, there was one team story that I vowed I would not ever watch. When *We Are Marshall* was released in 2006, I was sure it was a movie I could not handle. Why? Mainly because it was about death.

The film is based on the true story of the 1970 fatal plane crash that instantly killed 37 members of the Thundering Herd football team of Marshall University. The West Virginia town was dealt a crushing and tragic blow as it was left to deal with the devastating aftermath of the deaths of seventy-five people, which included the majority of the team, its coaches, athletic trainers, the athletic director, boosters, and the plane crew. It is not a movie I choose to watch over and over like some of the other football classics. Ultimately, I did watch it a total of two times. The first, I got pulled into it when it happened to be on the hotel TV of my honeymoon suite. The second was before writing this book. It is a good and well-made movie that I would watch again soon if it wasn't so hard to see young life come to such a sudden and tragic end. But it's worth watching again.

There are many things that resonated with me about *We Are Marshall*, and, in the end, it was impossible for me not to be moved by this story of love and the human spirit rising above death and destruction. Matthew McConaughey delivers an engaging and appealingly quirky performance as Jack Lengyel, the out-of-towner who takes on the nearly insurmountable task of helping the community heal as he keeps the football program alive.

The very beginning starts with Marshall's loss to West Virginia, some ardent fans traveling with the team while those at home are glued to their radios. One of the coaches' wives resigns herself to that fact that weekend time with her husband has just gone down the tubes. She knows that her husband and all the other coaches will be engrossed in game film until Monday.

We knew this well, too, our family.

We also knew, as the movie vividly captures, the sights and sounds of a football game. Marching bands, officials in black and white blowing their whistles, a crowd cheering on its feet, a pass lingering in the silent air, a punishing hit that could be heard so loud you felt it. It was all this and more that drew Jim Algeo to the game of high school football for the better part of his life.

One of the greatest moments of the *Marshall* film happens early on, when its President, Donald Dedmon, is giving heavy consideration to suspending the football program indefinitely. One of the team's surviving members, Nate Ruffin, played powerfully by actor Anthony Mackie, is passionate that the program must continue in order to honor his deceased teammates. Shouldering the effort to keep football alive at Marshall, he inspires the student body to join him in convincing the powers that be.

An overwhelmed Dedmon, who knows that there are big challenges ahead, accepts the strong consensus of the school community, but turns to Ruffin in exasperation. He just doesn't know how to start the rebuilding.

To Ruffin, it is clear. The first task is to find a coach. As he sees the known and unknown troubles that lay before them, Nate knows this decision is possibly the most critical.

In all my years as part of a football family, living with a head coach and being raised beside future head coaches, I know this to be true. And still, after all this time, it is nearly impossible to measure the value of a head coach or even define completely and accurately all that one is.

Yet this is the job that Jimmy believed God placed in his heart since the moment *Catholic Boy* Magazine was delivered to my grandparents' doorstep. Now that he had answered once and for all his question about the priesthood and knew he wanted Mickey as his wife and the woman who would help him raise a family, he set his sights on going after what he had wanted to do nearly his whole life.

With a week to go before the start of the school year in 1959, Jim returned to the mission he had declared was his to Mickey on the night he proposed to her. It was probably too late for that academic year and season, but, having left the West Catholic football practice he happened upon that hot August day, he had to give it a try.

The very next week, he was hired to teach typing at Cardinal Dougherty Catholic High School, where he became an assistant football coach. Less than two months later, he and Mickey married on October 17, 1959. He was about to start a family with the woman he loved, he was teaching high school students, and he was coaching football. It seemed that Jim had already accomplished all he wanted at the age of twenty-three.

Except, like the coach of the St. Polycarp High School football team in the pages of his boyhood magazine, he wanted to be the *head* coach. Still, 1959 would be a year of firsts for Jim and Mickey...first year of marriage, first teaching job, first coaching position, and buying the car seat for their first child.

By 1960, Chubby Checker had ignited a dance craze called "The Twist", John Fitzgerald Kennedy became President of the United States of

America, Rome hosted the Summer Olympic Games, the first troops were sent to Vietnam, and *Ben-Hur* was named Best Picture, taking home eleven Academy Awards. In the summer of 1960, Jimmy and Mickey were getting ready to bring home Maggie.

Mary Margaret Algeo was born in the summer of 1960. Though she had absolutely no reason whatsoever to think otherwise, my Nana Filliben prayed the Rosary every day that the child would not be born before the nine-month mark of June. Mom always found this comical. She had no need to worry. Maggie was born in late July and soon became Dad's weekend buddy as the assistant coach scouted various high school football teams playing on Fridays, Saturdays, and Sundays when Cardinal Dougherty wasn't. Except for occasionally joining in with the cheerleaders, the toddler sat and watched the game intently right alongside her father.

Fifteen months later, James Michael Algeo, Jr. was born during the football season of 1961. He was not the interested spectator my oldest sister was, scrambling from his seat in the stands and not at all engaged in the game my father was studying. He didn't know it then, but years later Jim Sr. would come to appreciate Jim Jr.'s ability to scramble quickly during football games.

Soon after young Jim was born, Mickey visited her parents with the news that she was expecting her third child.

"He's an animal!" my grandmother cried.

Eleven months after the birth of her brother, Mary Elizabeth Algeo was welcomed to the family in September of 1962. Mild and pleasant, she would climb up on the couch, content to watch her older siblings play rough and tumble with Dad on the floor. Jimmy and Mick were raising the children they had dreamed of having together. The building of the family was well underway.

All the while, Big Jim also dreamed of finding a head coaching job. Instead, in 1961, after two years at Cardinal Dougherty, he accepted a teaching and assistant coaching position at Sun Valley High School in the

Algeo family's new hometown of Aston, Pennsylvania. He remained there until 1965, when he accepted yet another teaching and assistant coaching job at Penncrest High School in Media.

That same year, Daniel John Algeo was born. He was named after both our grandfathers, Daniel Algeo and John Filliben. All Mom ever said about him as a little one was that he was just a good, happy baby. This made perfect sense to me because he grew into a good, happy boy who became my regular playmate and understood well my tendency to daydream.

While our family grew, now with four children, Big Jim's desire to land the head coaching position he had dreamed of since his *Catholic Boy* days only burned stronger. He applied whenever there was an opening within a reasonable distance, but, as the ten-year anniversary of his proposal to Mickey was approaching, he remained an assistant coach. The top position continued to elude him.

When I was born in March of 1967, named Mary Bridget Eileen after my great grandmother and my aunt, Dad was preparing for his third season as an assistant to the Penncrest High School Lions. A year later, however, he received a phone call from North Catholic High School in Philadelphia, where he had applied just two or three years before.

They wanted to know if Big Jim was still interested in the head coaching position of the football team there. At last, after nearly a decade of trying, he believed he was finally about to get his big break. His confidence that, at last, he would be the head coach he always wanted to be was heightened by a prediction someone made during his interview: the only way he wouldn't be hired was if Vince Lombardi himself applied.

Well, as these things happen, Vince didn't apply, and Dad didn't get the job.

Big Jim had a reputation for being patient, faithful, and able to keep his emotions in check when he was dealt a personal setback or disappointment. But this time, he cried. For the first time, he truly doubted that he would ever become a head coach of any team anywhere.

Now Mickey was raising five children in the spring of 1968. She had 7-year-old Maggie, 6-year-old Jim, 5-year-old Mary Beth, 3-year-old Danny, and a one-year-old who learned how to climb out of the playpen the first time she was put in it. On top of that, Algeo blessing number six was on the way, due that June.

Somehow, in the midst of caring for her family, chasing children, cooking meals, cleaning house, and doing laundry, she found the time to scour the newspaper every day. She was determined that Jimmy would not be devastated again.

Dad always called Mom from school during lunch, and, one day in late spring, she told him about a tiny little ad she had seen in the *Delco Times* that morning. Some high school named Lansdale Catholic was looking for a head coach for their football team.

Just a county to the north was a young Catholic high school which only years before sat atop the parish grade school three blocks down the street. Its meagerly-numbered inaugural graduating Class of 1953 was just 33 students. First known as Little Flower High School, named after the popular French saint, Therese of Lisieux, it moved to a new and bigger building on the corner of Seventh Street and Lansdale Avenue, where it opened its doors in September of 1960. From that time on, just over a decade from its humble beginnings, it was officially known as Lansdale Catholic High School.

"LC", as it affectionately became known, was the fruition of the clear-eyed vision and rolled-up sleeves of a small, balding, bespectacled priest named Monsignor Joseph Schade. The son of an upstate Pennsylvania brewery family who became the pastor of Lansdale's Saint Stanislaus Church enlisted the driven grade school principal, Sr. Therese Clare, as well as her team of workhorse Franciscan Sisters, to bring the dream of LC to life on nearly eighty acres of lush wooded land in a suburb of Philadelphia nestled among what seemed like boundless farmland at the time.

One of Lansdale Catholic's most distinct features were three fields that ascended like giant green steps from the bottom of the property along Seventh Street toward the building at the top of the street. A small, gentle bank rolled from one field into the next. Legend had it that the frugal Monsignor Schade bought a cow to graze those fields in the early days so he didn't have to pay for their upkeep.

Big Jim drove up the Seventh Street incline alongside those three fields as he arrived at LC for the first time in April of 1968.

Lansdale itself was a strange and foreign land to him that was an hour away from our house in Aston, Delaware County. Though encircled by farmland, it was a bustling town with its own newspaper, radio station, hospital, and train depot, as well as a downtown Main Street full of mom-and-pop shops sprinkled around a Woolworth. On one end of the town stood North Penn High School, one of the largest of its kind in the state. On the other end lie Lansdale Catholic.

Two men greeted him as he found LC and made his way into the interview. One was the principal of the school, Father William O'Donnell. The other was Paul Jefferis, the school's athletic director and boys basketball coach. It turns out that Jimmy and Father O'Donnell had already taught at Cardinal Dougherty, a school so big they didn't even know they were teaching in the same building almost ten years before.

After the interview, as Dad got into his car to drive the hour back to Aston, Paul turned to Fr. O'Donnell only seconds after he left the office. "We *gotta* take him, Father," he said to the priest who was silently nodding his head in agreement. They called him back for a second interview, introduced him to the pastor who had succeeded Monsignor Schade, Paul Cahill, and offered Jim Algeo the head coaching position at Lansdale Catholic High School.

The journey back to Aston began with brief ecstatic tears that quickly turned to thoughts racing with planning and preparing. The Catholic Boy and would-be priest was a head coach now. The dream was just beginning.

*

Having been raised on Irish songs and dancing, somewhere along the line I took note that one of the most striking and frequently covered ballads is a late 60's folk tune sung by Tommy Makem called "Four Green Fields." Heavy in symbolism, the lyrics pour with emotion, telling of pride and sons and loss and grief. The fields in the song are passionately cherished and, when one field is taken, a mother is left with just three green fields. Though there is violence and death as she seeks to reclaim her treasured lost field, the song ultimately ends in promise and hope.

After a decade of priceless experiences as an assistant coach, coupled with the disappointment of rejection after rejection in his quest to fulfill his dream of becoming a head high school football coach, Jim Algeo, Sr. now had his three fields. What he and Mickey and their growing family didn't have was a home in Lansdale.

In June of 1968, almost a month before expected, Mary Veronica Algeo came into the world and into our family. Mom always teased that it was the only time she was early. She also said that good things come in small packages. Little Ronni was small but special, and Dad soon learned that she could talk football with him and was extremely knowledgeable. By the time she was six, she was waking him up on Saturday mornings with handwritten plays for him and his team.

When Veronica was one-year-old, we moved to Lansdale. In the meantime, as Jimmy and Mickey searched for a new home for an entire year, Dad commuted from Aston to Lansdale, sometimes twice a day back and forth. He was teaching accounting and typing courses in the classroom by day, followed by daily football practices on the field to prepare for the weekend games.

In August of 1968, Big Jim met, for the first time, the Lansdale Catholic football team in the school cafeteria. There were about fifty boys sitting and chatting among the tables lined from wall to wall across the large room. One of them was a self-described "fifteen-year-old hot shot" named Patrick O'Hara, who was entering his junior year after having lettered as a defensive and tight end for the Crusaders.

"Coach Algeo walked in and introduced himself as the new head coach," recounted O'Hara. "Coming from the old regime, we didn't readily give our attention to him when he asked for it. And after about four, maybe five seconds, he let us hear 'The Voice.'"

Suddenly a loud voice boomed off the cafeteria walls.

"May I have your attention please!" roared the new coach.

"And it worked," according to O'Hara. "I mean our heads turned because we couldn't believe that voice came out of that little man. And he explained very briefly to us where he was from, what our schedules were, here is our equipment, see you at practice the next day."

Now the next day meant the official start of summer camp, a grueling mid-August high school football tradition in Pennsylvania right before the start of the school year. They generally consist of three-a-day practices, preparatory scrimmages, and relentless conditioning to ready for the fall season. Camp can be so brutal, particularly during the punishingly humid late days of summer, that even O'Hara quit during his freshman season because "it was too hard."

Patrick came back out again as a sophomore, as many of his classmates, like Tom Breslin and Larry Collins, were part of the team. He made it through camp and to the start of the season. Patrick and his teammates learned early on during camp of 1968 that the new regime under Coach Algeo was nothing they had yet experienced.

"Well, the first couple days of practice are pretty uneventful. You run, you do calisthenics, you run. You might push the sled around, and then you run some more. And it wasn't until the second or third day that we got to hear 'The Voice' a second time.

"The coach instructed us to do a rather unpleasant exercise, and one of our teammates showed his displeasure by calling on our Lord — and it wasn't in the context of a prayer."

"Who took the Lord's name in vain!" Big Jim hollered.

"We were dumbfounded. All he said was…" His voice trailed off, leaving the expression the young man used to be surmised.

The hot August practice came to a sudden halt. As sweat dripped off their faces, the team gathered around the small coach known as "Big Jim" simply because of the booming voice and large presence he impressed upon them from the start. O'Hara vividly recalled what the thirty-two-year-old man with dark wavy hair and a smattering of freckles said at that moment:

"And he stopped us right there and proceeded to explain what Lansdale Catholic football was going to be from now on. That everything we did on that field down there was for the glory of God. Everything we did down there was not about us. We were to respect each other, respect our parents, our coaches, and our teammates, our opponents. If we won, we won with our heads held high. If we lost, we congratulated our opponents. We held them with high regard because they beat us. If we were doing our best, they beat us as the better team.

"And that was the beginning of The Rare Breed."

It wasn't labeled as such then, but, that day, the seeds that grew the high school football power that Pennsylvania would come to know as the Rare Breed were planted on the three green fields grazed by Joseph Schade's cow. On them, thousands of young men wearing green and gold would come to practice over the next forty-four years as part of the Rare Breed tradition. It was sown following the tumultuousness of the late sixties, when a war was brought into our living rooms, when we witnessed the assassination of a President, his brother, and a beloved civil rights leader, and youth angst grew in the face of the breakdown of marriages and families. In a time when many young people in America turned to drugs and often violence, a new and refreshing counter-cultural attitude became rooted on an ordinary football field fifty miles from Philadelphia.

As the Rare Breed Tradition took root there and the Jim and Mickey Algeo family expanded, so grew another family, our Football Family. They were young men and their own families, all of us bonded by the excitement that is high school football — and our faith in God in a beautiful but troubled world not always ready or willing to receive Him. The culture that flourished on LC's three green fields became captured in a single motto that was known far beyond the boundaries of Lansdale: "Faith. Family. Football."

The latest used family car now drove us to new towns, communities of our opponents that soon became household names to our young ears. Conrad Weiser. Reading Central Catholic. Wyomissing. Exeter. Hamburg. Holy Name. And every July, it continued to take us to the little pink house in Sea Isle City for magical summers full of paddle ball tournaments, sunrises, and family time together. Just us. We knew that, upon our return, that part of the "Football Family" cycle that was summer camp would immediately begin, and that our parents would no longer totally be our own.

That was okay with us. We loved our Football Family, and we had found another sacred place on the football field.

~ FOOTBALL ~

CHAPTER FOUR

Sons of the Seventies

For whom the LORD loves He reproves,
Even as a father corrects the son in whom he delights.

~ Proverbs 3:12

After years of pursuing his vision, Big Jim was more than ready to bring on the first game and build his Rare Breed program. It was the summer of 1968. The average price of gas was 34 cents per gallon, a dozen eggs cost 53 cents, popular films included *The Odd Couple*, *Funny Girl*, and *Chitty Chitty Bang Bang*, The Beatles were singing "Hey Jude", and Dad was finally preparing for his first season as head coach.

Just as seeking and hiring a head coach is critical in the building of a successful program, so, in turn, is that coach's selection of his staff of assistants. Over the years, as Rare Breed football grew while nestled in a quiet neighborhood of Lansdale, several traditions flourished from their three green fields — and one of the most notable was the long line of green and gold men who stood beside Dad on the sidelines season after season.

The first Rare Breed assistant coach set the bar high, particularly for a young man. Fresh out of Bloomsburg University, he was handsome, affable, and youthful with a big smile and unforgettable laugh. For years, I believed he was a beer maker and was convinced that his beautiful wife, Ginny, was *That Girl*, Marlo Thomas. His name was Bernie Schaefer.

Probably because Bernie worked at the Lansdale beer distributor and almost everyone in America knew the beer jingle of the same name sung by the likes of Louis Armstrong, Lena Horne, and Paul Anka, I thought, as a child, Bernie had invented this famous beer. He didn't. He did, however, brand an enduring mark on the players of the early years.

According to early seventies Rare Breed lineman Mike Gildea, Bernie's impact was a lasting one. "He was the line coach, and he was the perfect counterpart to Mr. Algeo. He was in line with him, but yet when we separated to work on offensive line techniques, it was a different atmosphere. He had the same respect and so forth, but there was a little difference. I had a good rapport with him." Bernie's calm, easy style stood in contrast to the impassionedly demanding and significantly louder approach of the new head coach.

Thus, in addition to the assistant coach legacy at LC, another tradition became well-known — and rather quickly: the loud booming voice of the small but robust coach, as Patrick O'Hara and his teammates discovered before ever setting foot on the field with the man. When challenged to exceed expectation, the first ever Rare Breed team responded.

"He said maybe it's not for everybody here, and no one left the field that day," remembered O'Hara. "We were into the commitment and ...what that commitment entailed on the hot summer afternoons with mouths so dry you can't spit. Or on a November night, when your fingers are so cold, and you go down in the stance and your skin bleeds. But that was the deal we made, that was the commitment we made. Coach Algeo taught us every day, every game to respect and to play the best we could... to practice and practice until we did it right."

As they practiced, with opening night approaching, the local paper, *The North Penn Reporter*, cranked out its annual summer preview. Sports writer Dave Treffinger perfectly captured Dad's anticipation: "Lansdale

Catholic head football coach Jim Algeo can't wait for Saturday's football opener with Archbishop Carroll."

He also noted that the previous LC teams had struggled with timing the past few seasons. When the offense was strong, the defense was not. And, as in the year before, when the defense was on, the offense was lacking. The big question that Big Jim, Bernie, and the other coaches had to answer was, with fifteen lettermen returning, could the team generate an offense again?

Before Big Jim's baptismal year at the helm of LC football, Lansdale's trio of fields had already produced a legacy of offensive sparks despite its short history on the Pennsylvania high school football map. One was a small, spunky Italian player named George DiDomizio, who was the school's first quarterback and later became one of the community's most respected members and strongest school supporters.

A few years after the diminutive play caller came a 1959 graduate from Norristown by the name of Larry Glueck. A three-sport MVP at Lansdale Catholic, Larry went on to play for the Villanova Wildcats, with whom he won the Sun Bowl against Wichita State in 1961. He was signed by the Chicago Bears, where he played for three years under George Halas and was the first nickelback in the NFL. He became a teacher and a coach following a career-ending injury, and ultimately was appointed as the head coach of Fordham University.

At the heels of the Glueck years, a second Italian stallion stepped into the local limelight. He splashed onto the high school athletic scene as a freshman, earning starting positions on the LC football, basketball, and baseball teams. The Lansdale community was confident that Anthony Sandone would follow in Larry's footsteps, as multiple Division I scholarships offers rolled in for all three sports. Even as a promising NFL career shone on his future, Tony's parents did not want him to go to college. Instead, they insisted he take over the family business upon his graduation in 1964. Rather than pursue a collegiate and professional career, Anthony, at the age of eighteen, became a barber. He would later become a baker in Lansdale's Italian bakery.

Now, four years later, on the LC sidelines stood senior Chester Wisniewski, known to his friends and teammates as "Chet." At 6'2" and 185 pounds, he was backup fullback as a junior. This season, he was the starting left halfback and the second string quarterback to junior Steve Collins. As he and his teammates faced the challenge of jumpstarting the Rare Breed offense under the direction of their new coach on this first fall football evening, the names of the former offensive powerhouses were more than just a little well known to Chet and his teammates.

"I remember watching some of these guys play. I had an LC season ticket around 8 years old. Anthony Sandone was one of the most powerful running backs I have ever seen."

To teammate O'Hara, the young graduates that Wisniewski describes were "LC Legends": "Tony Sandone was always in the headlines of *The Reporter*. And Larry Glueck's name was almost sacred in any LC Football conversation."

As the new coach's nerves jounced, and his team stretched, ran drills, and prepared for their debut, the stands began to fill. It was September 14, 1968, and, for her sixth birthday, my sister Mary Beth attended a high school football game surrounded by Maggie, 8; Jimmy, also 6; Danny, 3; me, halfway past 1; and our mother, Mickey, who held 3-month old Veronica.

Getting them all in the family station wagon from Aston to Lansdale was no small victory for Mickey. As she gathered up the six of us, she went to the backyard to get young Jimmy, who was already engaged in a fall opener of his own. In addition, on his sister's sixth birthday, he was still trying to figure out how they were both the same age. It was not a question Mom could easily answer, so she turned her attention to rounding up her clan and getting them in the car.

"Jimmy, it is time to go to your father's game," she announced.

"Mom, I *play* football. I don't *watch* football!"

Mickey gave her son ten more minutes of playing football before returning to the yard. "You will not be missing your father's game." And with that, we were all on a car ride to Lansdale.

The first big move of the evening was maneuvering Chet to the quarterback spot. It turned out that Steve, slated to start at QB, was sick with a sore throat. In turn, Chet, Pat, and Company delivered a decisive season-opening win with an offensive effort that saw Wisniewski fire three touchdown passes in a 26-6 "trampling". Like the offensive firecracker he watched as an 8-year-old, the headlines would now frequently be his.

The first Rare Breed victory was a statement, sparking an inaugural season that was a winning one and that would sear an expectation deep into the bedrock of the Lansdale practice fields for the next two-thousand and more players.

Nowhere was this more well-known than in our own modest home in the borough's West Ward. A victory on a Friday night happily lingered over our family household like an Algeo family party for an entire weekend. A loss, however, especially if severe, entombed 526 Columbia Avenue like a funeral until Monday, when a chance to have another go at a win was resurrected after the school bell rang and practice resumed. Seeded in those early years were traditions that I was too young to remember as a child a few months shy of her two-year birthday, but I would come to know well later, as a daughter of football family life.

Just as she did that first ride, once we finally moved to Lansdale, Mickey continued a custom that would take place in the latest used vehicle as soon as we rounded the corner of our hometown street for the ten-minute drive to Pennbrook Middle School. As the fields of Lansdale Catholic did not consist of a stadium, our home field was a public school facility just blocks away from LC and minutes away from our house. It was humble compared to today's athletic buildings, but it was "home" to us, and we cherished it. On the way there, Mom would hand out the rosaries and lead us in a decade. The trip across town was too short to say the prayer in its entirety, mysteries and all.

Together, we said our one Our Father, ten Hail Marys, and a Glory Be, followed by Mickey's own prayer at the end: "Dear God, help us to win this game. No matter what, help the players to do their best, and let there be no injuries on either team." Amen. Ironically, at roughly the same time, in the LC locker room, Big Jim was leading the team in a decade of the rosary as well, always finishing with, "Our Lady of Victory, pray for us."

Away games in the Intercounty League definitely allowed for multiple Rosary recitations had Mickey been so inclined to pray the entire road trip. The other schools in the league were not close to Lansdale, most of them about an hour and a half drive up and over into Berks County. As a young child, I remember being plucked from my Saturday morning cartoon-watching, only to unwillingly be placed in the car to travel to what I remember the grownups calling, "God's Country." Mom saved the last ten minutes of those journeys for our weekly Saturday afternoon prayer.

The Rare Breed of the late sixties and early seventies I was too young to remember, though it is in these years the traditions were being planted. My memories during these years are murky at best, though one custom I recall learning first was what every player from every season experienced. "The Good One."

If the players lost the game, they silently reflected on the negative outcome and what hand they might have had in the loss. If they won, however, there was a routine that took place on the bus. At home, our family and fans would gather around and wait for it. Away, we would follow the bus until it cleared the premises of the hosting opponent.

Following their victory, once on the bus, the team would settle into their seats and await the players and coach being interviewed by local sportswriters or the town radio station, 1440 WNPV Radio. This whole process could take a while, but once they saw Big Jim finishing up his post-game remarks and heading toward the bus, they would silence themselves.

Often, he ambled at the bottom of the bus doorsteps for a few extra minutes, accepting congratulatory handshakes from fans, parents, sometimes former players. Most would agree he savored the winning moments for everything they were worth.

He would then climb up one step, then the second, then the last and stand at the front of the bus. Turning to his silent team, he would pump his fist in the air and let out a roaring "Good One!" The entire bus of players and the fans surrounding it would then go wild as the bus pulled away, driving off with a bunch of teenage boys reveling in the day's victory.

"They were two words as a Crusader that meant more than any speech," explained future Rare Breed player Kevin McCullagh of the Class of 1991, as he reflected on the "Good One!" tradition that would span over four decades.

The 1968 team had done its duty in posting the first ever "Good One." As 1970 rolled in, the first two seasons of Rare Breed had produced eleven of them over the last two years of the sixties and heralded in a new and intense program unique to area high school football. "Faith, Family, Football" was here to stay.

November of 1970 also brought the seventh child of James and Mary Margaret Algeo, Mary Frances.

Danny was convinced this child was going to be a baby brother, and he didn't believe him when Dad insisted Sister Number Five would be coming home the next day. He wasn't upset, he just thought Big Jim was joking, laughing at the notion there could possibly be *another* Mary in the house.

Now old enough, it was the first time I was aware that Mom had given birth, and we were welcoming a new member to our family. Nana Filliben came to stay with us to help out with the new baby for the week, and I distinctly remember her having to pull apart Danny and me from a slapping match as we jockeyed for position at the window to see our parents arrive home with our sister.

It was only then, when he saw her frilly dress and bright long-lashed eyes, did Danny finally accept that he might never be getting a younger brother. It didn't stop him or any of us from hanging out at her bassinet and admiring her all day, peering over its side waiting for her to wake up. We were amazed at how much she slept.

The fogginess of early childhood memories began to lift not long after the start of the seventies decade. At the time, Johnny Nash's "I Can See Clearly Now" was a radio favorite, and my own recollections of family life, including football, were being seen with greater sharpness and clarity.

I don't remember the team very much of the 1970 season, but they finished a strong 8-2-1. The young men on the team were household names on Columbia Avenue. One was Jim Flyzik, who some considered among the best athletes in LC history. Others were Joe Peck, Dennis Gawronski, and Tom Brown. Dad would reference Tom Brown many times in the future, due to him being small in stature, but tough and a fierce competitor — qualities he wanted all of his players to possess. I distinctly remember, in the fall of kindergarten, knowing that my dad was a high school football coach, our team colors were green and gold, and we were traveling to his games, home or away, near or far, hot, cold or rainy, like it or not.

I also learned what hatchets and stars were, as I watched my mom and older sisters paint dark green ones onto the helmets atop newspapers on the dining room table week after autumn week. Defensive players earned hatchets, offensive players earned stars, and, given the modest enrollment at Lansdale Catholic, most players earned both because we needed them to go both ways. I didn't understand it completely, but I knew the boys who performed well had a lot of hatchets and stars covering their helmets.

The weekly painting session was hardly the only contribution made by Mom. One of my earliest visions of football life was watching three giant drums filled with filthy dirty jerseys rolled in through the back door of our home each week. For many seasons, Mickey not only washed her own family's laundry, but the home and away jerseys of each of the players. Mind you, we didn't have a dryer until the mid-seventies, so, for years, the green grass of our backyard vanished amid shades of green, gold, and white shirts hanging from our clotheslines and flowing in the breezes of the fall months.

Another feat Mom pulled off every year was the annual Parent's Night that took place in early September at the end of summer camp. This evening event was a chance for Big Jim to talk to the parents about the team goals, values, and expectations, as well as come together to celebrate Mass with the families to mark the start of the season. It was followed by a reception with hot dogs, chips, ice cream, and chocolate milk, plus a birthday cake Mickey always baked for Dad — one big enough to feed a football team.

I never saw my mother complain about doing any of this. She happily painted helmets, washed uniforms, baked cakes, cooked hot dogs, hung jerseys, and went to every Rare Breed game except to deliver a child. To her, high school football was exciting, and she made sure from the very beginning we were all a part of that excitement.

What she did struggle with was the stark difference in social personalities between her and Dad. Mom was spontaneous, liked to get up and go, and enjoyed trying new things. Dad was more of a homebody who never really saw his own parents go on dates or go out for romantic evenings. As much as they both delighted in family functions and home life, the moments when it was just the two of them cherishing only each other were very, very few.

Mickey wasn't one to remain silent about her discontent with their contrasting visions of couplehood. The solution was simple. As the old saying goes, if Mom ain't happy, nobody's happy. Big Jim, as a loving husband would, ultimately went against his nature so that the two of them could enjoy dinner and a movie without a band of kids.

The real challenge was finding a babysitter savvy and skilled enough to watch seven children ranging from a toddler to a pre-adolescent. Enter Richard Trotter III, the son of Richard and Bernadette Trotter and the oldest of their thirteen children. He was also the starting cornerback for the 1971 Rare Breed of Lansdale Catholic.

Known by Dad for his ability to manage his own siblings, as well as the young brood of Paul Jefferis, the LC Athletic Director and Head Boys Basketball Coach, Richard went to great lengths to get me not be scared at bedtime. He repeatedly swiped his finger through a candle flame in an effort to entertain me so that I would forget my parents were gone. He had a great manner with people. He would later be voted by his classmates in the spring of 1972 to become a member of Student Council, earned Class Valedictorian, and still later, a West Point Graduate.

The 1971 season was a rough one. First, Richard sustained an injury that required surgery. Second, the winning roll stalled, and the Green & Gold mustered just two victories. I don't have much memory of the football statistics exactly, but I was close to kindergarten age when I was recognizing more and more that what happened on the Rare Breed football field had a direct connection to the mood of our living room, the dining room table, and even a car ride.

In fact, at that age, counselors conducted routine testing for all the students entering school, and we were each asked to draw anything we wanted. I didn't draw our house, a flower, the family dog, or even my mom. I drew a picture of my dad, in his coaching gear, throwing a football in a typical quarterback pose. I was happy with the final product and asked the woman if I could keep the pencil sketch. She had to keep it for the files and the parental conference, but my mom retrieved it for me because the tester recalled I had wanted it so badly.

I impressed on the counselor that I was no fan of school, where I cried a lot upon my arrival because I missed hanging out with my mom all day. I had been perfectly happy with our previous arrangement of waking up when I wished, watching *Mighty Mouse*, *Underdog*, and the *Banana Splits*, and doing everything alongside Mom. But I went on to learn my colors and shapes and sight words and days of the week like every other five-year-old. I also learned a word I would guess is not on the vocabulary list of most kindergarten students.

Undefeated.

*

Like most five-year-olds, I was obsessed with the things of great importance at that time. What was I going to be for Halloween? How long until my birthday? What am I getting for Christmas? Holidays, parties, and toys — these were matters of importance. Except for these priorities and high school football, I was pretty much in the dark when it came to all that was happening outside our home in the West Ward of Lansdale that year.

And a lot was going on.

Governor George Wallace was shot, Watergate dominated the news, and Mark Spitz won seven gold medals in an Olympiad that was terrorized in Munich. Hurricane Agnes swallowed up much of Pennsylvania, digital watches were introduced, and people could now somehow play games on their television sets. *The Godfather* was released, *The Brady Bunch* reigned supreme on television, everybody was singing Don McClean's "American Pie", and football fans were witnessing the Miami Dolphins roll into history as they won the Super Bowl with an unbeaten record. To date, they are the only professional team to have gone undefeated.

Our family continued to make our way down the shore year after year for the annual pre-football season vacation. In 1972, with our return from North Wildwood, Big Jim looked to begin his fifth season at Lansdale Catholic. Our family, having officially moved to the borough on June 18, 1969, was not only comfortably settled in, but still confidently growing. Between Columbia Avenue and the three green fields, we were part of Dad's off-season as much as we were the on-season, and the little high school at Seventh Street and Lansdale Avenue became a second home.

Instead of going to local playgrounds, Dad usually took us to the LC gym, fields, and weight room to let off steam — and to give Mom a breather from all of us other than shopping at the grocery store. One of the first places I ever played as a young girl was a sort of "cage" that housed the weights in the boys' locker room. My siblings and I would take the pins from the stack of weights and try to beat each other lifting and pressing what we could. We also played on the mats, the court, the stage, the stands, and the fields there, and it opened us up to the wide world of sports and all the wonderful things it can bring.

Upon returning to summer camp in August, something not so wonderful happened to Dad. He came home one night so sick that Mom took him to the emergency room. Somehow, Big Jim had contracted mononucleosis, otherwise known as "the kissing disease". The local paper joked that the illness seemed more appropriate for his players than their mentor. Still, it was serious enough that he was not permitted to teach or coach until he was in the clear from communicating the disease to others. With Big Jim out of commission, the reigns of another grueling summer camp were handed to Rare Breed Assistant Coach, the handsome and likable Bernie Schaeffer. While he was typically not quite the yeller Dad was, Bernie ran an extremely tough and rugged summer camp. He was intent on making sure the team was prepared when Dad returned to practice.

During the grueling sessions, players were not to remove their helmets unless instructed. Not even two days into camp, Bernie saw one of them sitting on the sideline with his helmet by his side. The young assistant did not realize the new boy was sick with a virus, and, as the player looked at him with his head and one eye turned away from him, Bernie hollered, "Hey you in the daydream world! Helmet on and back on the field!"

Following the outburst, there was an awkward silence that descended upon the group of teenage boys before one of them spoke out.

"Coach Shaeffer," said Larry Collins, the player's cousin. He knew his kin wasn't looking at Bernie funny. "He's blind."

He was Mike Wisniewski, brother of Chet, who had introduced the Rare Breed quarterback tradition to the area with a 3-TD win five years earlier, and he was, in fact, legally blind. Though he wanted to go to LC, his parents sent him to North Penn's middle school because, as a public school, they had resources for the visually-impaired. Still, they agreed he could transfer if he made the honor roll. Not only did he get the grades, but he would transfer and eventually earn the starting position as an offensive tackle as a sophomore. Because he used only his peripheral vision to play, he took his stance with his head turned in such a way that his opponents did not know where he was looking. Even though he was so thin that his teammates called him, "Sticks", he was not to be trifled with — nor was the rest of the squad of '72.

Newcomer Mike was flanked by a strong cast of teammates, our former babysitter, Rich Trotter and a host of classmates: Mike Gildea, Barry McCarron, Joe Ritinski, the DeFinis Brothers, Ron DiCola, Kevin Heppler, Mike Folkes, Nick Thee, and Jimmy Boaman. One of them, the speedy Chip Zawoiski, earned All-Intercounty League honors, as did Barry and Ron, with an amazing 25-touchdown season. A fourth All-Intercounty award winner, Jim Boaman, helped define the Rare Breed brand of defense the area would come to know. When facing the leader of a devastating defense, opposing teams could seldom run or pass the ball with Boaman's frequent disruption of their backfield.

They were all led by a small quarterback who did not have speed. Rather, the diminutive John Wagner relied heavily on spirit and savvy. At 5 feet and 7 inches, Wagner was, like Wisniewski, a transfer. He was not local, coming with his family to Lansdale all the way from Grand Rapids, Michigan. He also brought leadership and intelligence, with a knack for reading defenses and finding open receivers with great consistency. Big Jim discovered that young Wagner also found a way to win.

Wagner's first encounter with the small Lansdale school, however, was somewhat tentative.

"I came from a big school, Grand Rapids Central Catholic. We came here and my dad kept talking it up. I got here and said...what are we getting ourselves into?"

Wagner distinctly recalls a moment halfway through his junior year when Big Jim decided to change the offensive scheme. Instead of calling them all in front of the chalkboard with X's and O's, he burst into the cafeteria where the boys were sitting and ripped open his jacket, exposing a tee-shirt with one of Jim Jr.'s favorite cartoon characters front and center.

The young men were puzzled, laughing at the display, and wondering if their head coach had gone mad. How did this childhood cartoon character have anything to do with their success as a team? But soon, they saw the rewards of the sudden and unusual decision to revamp the entire offensive plan midway through the season — a funny-looking cartoon favorite now the name of their offense.

"Coach had the instinct to do that," explained Wagner. "He picked the perfect offense for the players. I could have never played quarterback in any other offense."

The change worked because the small but heady quarterback from The Great Lakes State led the Green and Gold into a glorious season, picking off opponent after opponent until they earned the rare distinction of being the only undefeated team in LC history, finishing 10-0. They were a powerhouse on offense, averaging almost 30 points a game and only allowing only about 8 per game on defense. The group also continued the tradition of Dad's teams routinely being one of the top defensive teams in the area.

The players nearly unanimously agreed that it was the attitude of the seniors the year before, when they struggled to pick up a win and went a dismal 3 and 7, that directly impacted the 1972 winning season. Big Jim often referred to that squad as his favorite team, saying he learned so much from them, as they started out 1-6. Through hard work and determination, they improved significantly throughout the second half of the season, setting the groundwork for 1972.

"They never gave up," Dad would often say about the squad that refused to be demoralized.

After I learned the definition of "undefeated", and I understood that, like the NFL's Miami Dolphins, our Green and Gold team had not lost a single game all season, I started to become more interested in the Lansdale Catholic football team and its adventures. Many of these surnames I learned of in the seventies would become Algeo family household names for years to come, as brothers from the O'Haras, the Wisniewskis, the Walshes, the Wagners, the Folkeses, the Ritinskis, the Roddys, the DeFinises, the Collinses, the Trotters, and many other families would become players and some of them even coaches over a span of decades.

Still, it was the season of 1975 that was the personal game-changer for me. It was then that I first became emotionally invested in the team's players and their wins and losses. To this day, I credit it to a single player whose last name I have not seen before or since. He was fast, athletic, and could jump really high. More than that, he was tall and handsome and had perfect seventies hair. It was just the right style and just the right length. His name was Mike Purcell, and he was "Sunshine".

It was 1975, and my crush on Sunshine ignited what had once been a complete lack of interest in our high school football team only years before. Now I paid attention, began to understand the basics of the game, the rules, the positions, and, even more importantly, what a hard-fought victory and a "Good One!" meant to a group of teenage boys who donned their pads and helmets every weekend in front of a passionate Lansdale crowd.

One thing I also noticed around this age was that my father, as both a teacher & coach, would often yell without warning when correcting a young man, starting with a booming "Son!"

"Son! Tuck your shirt in!"

"Son! Don't ever be double dumb!"

"Son! *Get after it!*"

In all the years I would watch him coach, I never heard one single person object to him addressing them this way. Big Jim truly saw his mission of those in his charge aligned with that of their parents, and he deeply respected the care that was entrusted by them to him. These boys were like sons in many ways. Even the girls in Chet Wisniewski's bookkeeping class called the star player, "Jim's son."

Our one-time babysitter Rich explained that what was done in the classroom or on the football field continued the work of many parents at home.

"From the time I got up in the morning, I was in an environment where the values that were taught to me by my mother and father were reinforced throughout the day. In the classroom, you learned about the faith. But on the field is where you applied the faith under adverse conditions."

As the undefeated team moved on, the *Faith, Family, Football* dynasty kept on growing in Lansdale. In 1973, calling themselves her "godfathers", all the boys on the team, in football family fashion, signed a ball to welcome the birth of their coach's daughter, our youngest sister Mary Eileen, born September 19.

And, in 1975, Big Jim's own and first-born son would enter the doors of Lansdale Catholic and become part of the tradition deeply rooted in its three green fields.

*

In the early seventies, almost two hundred miles and a three hour drive from Lansdale, a football story was waiting to be told. There, in Alexandria, Virginia, an African-American high school football coach and his staff worked together to overcome challenges as they integrated their team in a racially charged climate. Their journey is recounted in the popular film, *Remember The Titans*. I won't say one hundred percent sure that this is my favorite football film, but it just may be.

The movie begins with the white Coach Bill Yoast, a beloved and respected hometown coach whose wife has left him because of his obsession with football, being displaced by the school board with the black Coach Herman Boone, a no-nonsense and driven leader who asks the former coach to come on board and help him guide the team through the changing times. Together, they navigate the Titans on their adverse journey and onto a path toward the state championship game.

There are many myths, misconceptions, and misunderstandings to be overcome among both the players and the coaches on their mission, and one scene that impacted me in particular illustrates how they help each other recognize them. Coach Yoast, believing that Boone is too hard on one of the young black players, the fumble-prone Petey Jones, goes out of his way to coddle him, speaking to him in a softer, gentler manner than toward the other players.

Boone confronts Yoast, helping him to see how treating the young player differently than everybody else is truly hurting him. He acknowledges that he understands that he himself can be very tough, but he is that way to everybody. No one is to get preferential treatment on his team. Everybody is to be treated with equal dignity and respect — and equal harshness.

For Big Jim, this same philosophy permeated his growing football program. In fact, even as individual players began to shine and deliver outstanding performances, it was clear to all that the Rare Breed's success always came down to what they did as a team. Even a standout like LC Class of 1973 Alumnus Chip Zawoiski, who was the Division III Player of the Year while playing for National Champion Widener University and was invited to try out for the Philadelphia Eagles, would see his uniform go to the next man. While other places would retire jerseys that the exceptional athletes wore, Dad refused to implement such a policy. Every young man would have a chance to be better than the player that wore that number before him. As we reached the mid-seventies, our family knew that our brother would soon have that chance.

Young Jim's football career, which had begun in our backyard in Aston, relocated to Lansdale when he was just seven years old. He entered Saint Stanislaus Grade School as a third grader, which was just about the time Mr. Anthony Sandone, the former LC star athlete who gave up multiple collegiate scholarships to maintain the family business, decided to start a local football program for area youth.

And, while the former LC powerhouse running back and Class of 1964 alum had not found the NFL, the NFL did find him. During the 1973 Thanksgiving Washington Redskins' win over the Detroit Lions, a 10-minute documentary featuring Tony and his 50-pound squad representing the Saints of St. Stanislaus Parish aired on national TV. The piece was perfectly and masterfully narrated by the legendary John Facenda. By this time, Big Jim had learned of Tony's passion for football and invited him to join the Rare Breed coaching staff while at the annual Parish Summer Festival years earlier.

Tony Sandone was now coaching boys as young as ten in the afternoon and teens as old as eighteen in the evenings. One was his own son, my classmate, Tony, Jr. Another was our brother, James Algeo, Jr. My young eyes saw, over the next few years, that it is one thing to be called "son", but another to be a son, and still another to hold the title of the junior. When, in *Remember The Titans*, Coach Boone declared he was rough on every team member, in my life I saw even greater expectation and stronger demand placed on the shoulders of the sons of the coaches. At least on the Rare Breed football fields.

Jimmy entered LC as a freshman in 1975 with the distinction that he shared the same name of his father, the head coach of the football team. That might have been tough enough to find a way to deal with. To top it off, his older sister was a name area sports fans would only ever know as simply Maggie. She didn't even need a last name for people to know who she was.

It wasn't just that she was a Top Ten student throughout her years at Lansdale Catholic. She was a scholar-athlete who garnered many individual awards and honors in field hockey, tennis, softball, and basketball, leading her squad to the only Pennsylvania Final Four appearance the girls hoops team ever saw. There were few mornings that Dan and I opened *The North Penn Reporter* over our bowls of cereals without Maggie being on the front of the sports page. Twenty years later, when I helped my best friend move into her new Bucks County home where the former owner had left much behind, we found much of it wrapped in newspapers with articles and photos of Maggie.

Now it was Jim's turn.

It was hard for us to know what it would be like to have one of our brothers as part of the team Dad yelled at day in and day out. What kind of player would Jim be? What if he had a bad game and they lost? Would he be able to live up to being the head football coach's son?

Jimmy forged ahead into the unfamiliar territory and became part of the Rare Breed program. He had already answered the question that he had wanted to play, which he had known since he was a small child. He then answered the question of which position by joining that unique brand of boys known as the quarterbacks.

During his sophomore year, he was playing significant time on the junior varsity team, where former players John Wagner and Joe Ritinski joined Anthony Sandone in molding the JV players and preparing them for varsity. The small but tough team had established its reputation as a competitive force among the Bucks, Berks, and Montgomery Counties of Pennsylvania and a respectability that was about to put them face to face with the giants of Lansdale — the Knights of North Penn High School.

Regardless of the drastic difference in size, the community had talked about a crosstown matchup for years now, and, finally, on Saturday, November 13, 1976, LC's David was about to start slinging on the home field of NP's Goliath. Only a sophomore, Jimmy was not yet ready for primetime, but was the Rare Breed's first string?

The North Penn Reporter sent their staff to cover the big game. I will always remember the photograph on its front pages, a big black and white with the official tossing the coin in between the schools' two sets of captains. For Lansdale Catholic, in the middle of the field stood senior quarterback Jeff Crawford and wide receiver Matthew Walsh.

Matt was the younger brother of Bill, who had been part of the undefeated team of '72 and the oldest in a line of six Walsh boys that would ultimately play over a span of fifteen years. To Big Jim, Matt was a godsend of an athlete. To the Rare Breed, he was the model teammate. But for the female student body, with his blond wavy hair, slender and muscular physique, and bright blue eyes, he was a dreamboat with a kind heart that also burnt an incredible competitive fire.

I was in third grade when I watched Matt lead the team on to the field to battle a school three times LC's size. Mom and Veronica, who was overcoming a bout with asthma, found a warm spot in the press box that was perched above the North Penn Stadium, while my cousins and I ran around the fields behind the stands during the game. Whenever the Rare Breed took possession, we would run over to the fence around the field to get a view of the offensive outcome.

It was slow-going for a while until Bart Lopez, our dynamic running back, broke free of the pack and burst for a long run into the end zone. In the predominantly North Penn press box, Mom and Veronica found themselves to be the only ones cheering the game-winning touchdown.

It would take a few years, but the friendly crosstown rivalry would resume one day. But for now, we would revel in the "Good One" all Saturday afternoon and evening. Our house on Columbia Avenue took its cue from the Algeo family tradition of celebrating in true Irish fashion as happy family, friends, and neighbors streamed into our home all day to toast David's defeat of our hometown Goliath. Even a brief glance at the

Knights' successful history from then until now meant such a victory was not to be taken lightly.

In the months after the win, Matt Walsh and the Class of 1977 graduated, Bernie Schaeffer moved on from the coaching staff, and a new shot of assistants was infused into the flourishing program. Anthony Sandone, Joe Ritinski, and John Wagner now became part of the Rare Breed think-tank. Poised with their clipboards and pens, Maggie and Mary Beth were given the duty of team statisticians. Lastly, Danny was now the official ball boy of the Lansdale Catholic Football Team.

As the seventies inched toward their end and the Rare Breed of Lansdale was nearing its ten year anniversary, the boys who practiced daily on the second green field became part of a growing brotherhood connected by many common experiences. As Bob Gillies, who as a senior led the team in the fall of 1977 and who Big Jim described as one of his toughest players, recalled:

"There are many things Coach would say that we all remember.

"One billion Chinese don't give a damn what happens on this football field. It only matters to us what happens here.'

"Pressure makes a diamond.'

"Don't ever be double dumb.'

"But the most important thing that connected us was that we were taught to count on each other. Even if we weren't friends, we were teammates. The Classes of '78 and '79 did not blend well together, but on the field, we literally fought for each other, especially against Bristol. On the field, we were one."

That same sense of unity went beyond just that year's Rare Breed, and, before 1977 was over, when Maggie was a junior, our family got a taste of something very special that takes place for a rare few in the world of high school sports. For the first time in school history, a girls basketball team made it all the way out to Hershey Arena for the State Championship Tournament. I was a fourth grader in Mrs. Colgan's class at Saint Stanislaus.

The excitement in our house was incredible. I woke up that spring morning, and, instead of putting on my school uniform, got dressed to take a family car ride halfway across the state of Pennsylvania to watch a high school basketball game, the prestigious Final Four. I came down the stairs that Thursday morning full of pride and anticipation.

My mom greeted me in the dining room as I hopped off the last step.

"Where is your uniform? Why aren't you ready for school?" she asked.

I looked at her like she was joking, much the same way Danny had looked at our dad when he had announced we had a new baby sister instead of a brother. I didn't say anything, as I am sure my face said it all. *Are you crazy? What are you talking about? Our team is going to states!*

Mom read my mind. "Oh, you thought you were going to the game today. I'm sorry, Bridge, you have to go to school."

To me, almost ten years old now, this idea that I would not be going to watch our sister in the state tournament was nothing shy of sheer madness. For almost three years, we had all as a family attended nearly every game. We walked the three blocks from St. Stan's to the home ones after school. We got our homework done early and crammed into the family wagon to go the away ones. And, in the past few weeks, we went to strange towns as the girls advanced, one game after another, against teams we never heard of.

All I had heard as we journeyed from gym to gym these past few weeks was "States. We might be going to States!" And now here we were, going to States — only I wasn't going!

To this day, I suspect Big Jim was mostly behind this decision. He had long expressed his policy that we were not to miss school, practice, games, work unless we were essentially dying, or at least had mono or were giving birth to a child. It didn't matter because, in the end, I went back upstairs and begrudgingly put on my blouse and plaid uniform, found matching green socks from the family sock box, and sulked in the back seat of the car for the seven minutes across town to Stan's.

As I got out, I remember the words my mom said: "You can go next year when your sister will be a senior."

The thing is, when it comes to State Championships, if there ever is one, there very rarely is a next year. In this case, there was not. Still, there was great joy as Maggie and her teammates returned from Hershey, Pennsylvania with a giant blue and gold trophy for being the third best team in their division in the state. It was a wonderful time, and we were always proud of that run.

From then on, I realized that there was someone in our growing household always going after some kind of sports championship.

The next trophy that would then be pursued was one engraved with the Intercounty League football title in 1978. At the time, Pennsylvania football did not have a state championship system, so, unlike Maggie, Jimmy's team would never have a chance at Hershey. Their one shot at high school glory and a championship crown would be to best the teams of Berks County.

In the year 1978, Dad had been head coach for ten years now, and Maggie was the first in our family to graduate from Lansdale Catholic. Our living room was one of many continuing to watch *Happy Days* and *Little House on the Prairie*. Popular films were *Grease, Animal House, Star Wars*, and *Saturday Night Fever*. The Bee Gees were singing disco hits from its soundtrack, like "Night Fever" and "Stayin Alive", while Paul McCartney and the Wings sang "With A Little Luck" off their latest album — although for two years now, Danny was still regularly singing "Silly Love Songs" from their last album.

That year, the average cost of a house was $54,800, a gallon of gas was 63 cents, and a dozen eggs were sold for approximately 48 cents. If you wanted to buy an 8-track player, it would cost you about $169, while you paid anywhere from $6.49 to $11.99 for a set of *Star Wars* pajamas. Sadly, Pope Paul IV passed away, giving way to the first Pope John Paul.

Thirty days later, he suddenly died, and Pope John Paul II was presented to the world.

As things were changing all around us, it seemed our family traditions mattered even more. Our family vacations down the shore right before football season remained uncompromisingly intact. The pink house in Sea Isle was still the hub for our ever growing extended family — and I, at eleven years old, had still yet to ever sleep in a bed there.

It was around that time that I noticed a quiet ritual Big Jim would conduct almost every single summer we pitched camp on the beaches of the Jersey shore. He generally waited until the young ones were out of the water and on ratty old blankets eating our sandy lunches with iced tea in paper cups from a massive thermos. Then he would wade out to into the ocean, a little more than waist high, where he would lie on his back and drift among the gently rolling waves.

I did not know until well into adulthood that this tradition was a means of simply savoring life and family in the short two weeks between the intense offseason and the brutal, demanding camp and the lineup of weekend games about to begin upon our return. And this season, in particular, with his son taking the snaps as the starting quarterback, was one like no other.

Surrounding young Jim were the self-proclaimed "Werewolves of London", a nickname born of a song that became a sort of anthem for the squad whose connections to Rare Breed past were strong. John Walsh, brother of Matthew and Bill. Owen Collins, brother of Larry and cousin to Chet and Michael Wisniewski. Jimmy Wagner, brother of John and Freddy Wagner. Michael Trotter, brother of Richard and Terry Trotter. The Lansdale Catholic football roster was starting to read like Biblical genealogy. Even so, fresh new Rare Breed blood bulked up the LC starting lineup as well. By the end of August camp, it was clear that John Saldutti, Mike O'Brien, Donny Drakas, Larry Nacarella, Vince Benvinuto, Joe Chrismer,

Ralph Guliano, and the "Werewolves" of 1978 started shaping up to be possible contenders for the league crown.

The one team that stood in its way, according to the preseason rumblings in our house, was Conrad Weiser. Located an hour and a half away, the Scouts hailed from Robesonia, Pennsylvania. Their school namesake was one of the first teams' names I learned, mostly because it was unusual to me. What was Conrad Weiser?

Mom explained that the proper question was *who* was Conrad Weiser? It turns out he was born in Germany in the late 1600s and came to America in 1710 with his family. So impactful was he, a local school district named after him was created in 1956. He was a Pennsylvania Dutch pioneer, interpreter and a diplomat between the Pennsylvania Colony and Native Americans. He was also a farmer, soldier, monk, tanner, judge, and a man whose name drove the Werewolves of London to work harder than the day before on the layered practice fields of Lansdale.

The Rare Breed would see one non-league and six league opponents before the highly anticipated matchup with the favored Scouts. Big Jim made it clear to his team, in no uncertain terms, that each of those games was just as important as the scheduled Game #8, which preseason sports writers picked would decide the Intercounty League Championship. And before each of those games, my sisters and I were introduced to what every high school athlete would know as "psych music."

There were three stories in our home in Lansdale, and Jimmy's room was straight up the second set of fourteen stairs of the six-bedroom house. It became ritual for him to eat a bowl of cereal before a game, then disappear behind the closed door of this third floor bedroom. From the second floor, at the bottom of the steps, we learned the words of nearly every Rolling Stone song as they spun on a twelve-inch vinyl record on the stereo in Jimmy's room.

As the schedule meandered its way to the projected showdown with Conrad Weiser, high school football took a series of twists and turns it is often known to do through the months of fall. Jimmy and his teammates were heading into the sixth game of the season with four wins, plus a loss against its single non-league opponent. Then came the Exeter Eagles, a team that lived about an hour west of Lansdale.

Dad, Jim, and the Werewolves of London found themselves down 0 to 14 at halftime. With Weiser and other formidable opponents still on the schedule, the Green and Gold could not afford a loss. They battled back to tie the game, 14-14, thus keeping their Intercounty League Championship hopes alive.

Two games later came the Conrad Weiser Scouts. What was to be the clash of the Intercounty League Titans ended in a landslide in favor of the Rare Breed, 23-0.

We all learned at a very young age in our household that you don't celebrate a victory you haven't won yet. I am guessing in large part to the Wyomissing Spartans, who, just like the Exeter surprise, burst to a 14-0 lead over our team. This is the year I learned what it meant to be a "spoiler".

Spoilers don't have a shot at winning the whole ball of wax, but they sure can come along and destroy a contender's hopes. Wyomissing was looking to do just that, but it would not be this day. Jimmy led a come-from-behind win that left a 29 to 14 final score shining on a scoreboard over a field of jubilant teenage boys wearing green and gold uniforms.

There were several outstanding players that day, as there had been all season. Against the Spartans, Tom Famularo rushed for 181 yards on 14 carries, including runs of 57, 46 and 22 yards, mostly escorted by Owen Collins, a devastating blocker and tremendous runner himself. John of the Walsh line, an all-league nose tackle, caused a fumble on a punt return, allowing the Crusaders to score and lead at half time, 15-14. Ultimately, they dominated the second half behind the strong offensive line of Albert Parambo, Jeff Olimpo, Charlie Murgia, Mike Murphy, and two sophomores — the gargantuan Marty Roddy and massive Bob Klein.

With the win, they had clinched the title. The defense finished number one in the area, allowing only 7 points per game, and number two in offense, posting an average of 25 points a contest.

Dad couldn't say it, but he didn't have to. We all knew and, years later, Joe Ritinski, the undefeated season of '72 member who later assisted and ultimately announced games on local radio, would:

"I truly believe the team wouldn't have won that championship without Jimmy's leadership as quarterback. He was focused, executed well, and was an extremely hard worker. In fact, he was voted as the team's Most Dedicated Player his senior year."

A week later, the Werewolves of London, in their final game against Kutztown, squeezed out one more win to end the season. And that would-be spoiler Wyomissing went on to defeat Conrad Weiser that same day. Besides the new vocabulary word, "spoiler", I also learned the saying, "Never say never." A pre-season write-up in August that predicts this team or that team to win will become a yellow newspaper whose pages will be used for firewood, putting away Christmas presents, or wrapping moving items one day. But the memory of a championship season will never be put away for an entire lifetime. It lives in the heart, like other family memories, forever.

A personal victory had also been won. Facing the challenge and pressure of being the head coach's firstborn son, Jimmy prevailed decisively. He was the starting quarterback and a member of the 1978 Intercounty League Championship Football Team. And, as he moved out to go to Widener University, formerly the Pennsylvania Military Academy Dad had attended twenty years before, Danny was now moving on to the Lansdale Catholic fields.

But not before another winning occasion called for celebration.

I sat on my bed one Thursday evening when Big Jim and Mick appeared at the door at a little after 8 o'clock. Both were smiling and wearing coats. Mom had one hand on her round belly and the other on a small suitcase by her side.

"We are going to the hospital now," declared Dad.

Jumping off the bed with joy, I ran over to say goodbye. After our happy exchange, they turned, walked down the hallway, and called the little house phone tucked in the corner of our dining room just over an hour later with an announcement. John Patrick Algeo, the ninth child of Jim and Mickey Algeo, was born.

Danny got his little brother.

Never say never.

CHAPTER FIVE

Sons of the Eighties

May He grant you your heart's desire
And fulfill all your counsel!

~ Psalm 20:4

As the small Catholic high school of an Eastern Pennsylvania suburb of Philadelphia, physical size was not something we were known for or accustomed to. There were very few "big" things in our world. One of those things, however, became a huge part of our family album.

Three long blocks down the street from Lansdale Catholic stood Saint Stanislaus School and, across the street from that, its big, beautiful church. Someone once told me that there is no parish church in the entire Archdiocese of Philadelphia that is as large as the one at the corner of Main Street and Lansdale Avenue. I don't know if that's true or not, but I do know that it is one tremendous church that can seat a *lot* of people.

Big Jim and Mick established the policy that each of their children were to begin to go to Mass at Saint Stan's every Sunday once we entered the first grade. Not understanding much that was going on or being said, I spent most of my hour there studying all its glorious details, from the big blue and stained glass windows to the white lights suspended from its wooden ceilings. For many young years, I read the words and sayings all around the church, convinced some of them were misspelled even though they were just Latin. Hands down, in all my intense examination, nothing in Saint Stanislaus Church was as eye-catching as the commanding black cross and its sculpture of Jesus right in the center of the wall behind the altar.

My brothers and sisters and I were raised seated in one of its rows and rows of shiny wooden pews stretched across the entire church, long and wide. Our family easily filled one pew when we attended Mass together. This, very often, was not the case, however. With five Masses being celebrated every Sunday, we would usually leave Columbia Avenue in shifts, and you caught a ride with Mom, Dad, or one of the older ones who had gotten their driver's license. Saint Stanislaus Church became a familiar house to not only our Sunday call to worship, but for our baptisms, confessions, Communions, Confirmations, graduations, and weddings. Placed high above the football field and the shore, it was our number one sacred place where we celebrated joyous life occasions from birth.

Our grand and spirited clan came together there once again as the seventies came to end and the next decade waited in the wings to bring its own moments of history, fads, devices, music, and, of course, movies. In March of 1980, we were excited to see our oldest marry as Mary Margaret Algeo and Michael deMarteleire exchanged vows front and center of our lovely church, under its magnificent cross. Like our parents, money was tight for the young couple, so a simple reception followed at the small Knights of Columbus hall just a few blocks away.

Again, size didn't matter, and this happy family event reminded us what can be done with a little resourcefulness and a lot of heart. It was modest but mighty and memorable, and the afterparty back at Columbia Avenue lasted hours into the early morning. With our first family wedding, the eighties were rung in, along with Ronald Reagan, the eruption of Mount St. Helen, the death of John Lennon, and the birth of Big Jim and Mickey's first grandchild, Michael deMarteleire, Jr.

It also steamrolled in the Rare Breed's first taste of, ironically, that thing called size in the form of senior Martin Roddy, Jr., standing six feet and eight inches tall and weighing in at 250 pounds. As a sophomore, he had the job of protecting our brother Jim on the way to the 1978 Championship.

Marty was quiet, humble and an extremely hard worker. With his size and strength, he was a punishing blocker. One of his biggest problems, however, was finding a teammate, comparable in size, to help in pre-practice stretching. He found a partner in fellow sophomore Bob Klein, the center on the 1978 squad. Bob was 6'1, 230 lbs., and by far, he was the nearest in stature to Marty. When the coaches had the players stretch their legs, Marty would put his foot on Bob Klein's shoulder, rather than on his back like the other players, who would bend over to allow for full muscle extension. The unique sight between the team's two biggest players would amuse the players and coaches those first few weeks of practice.

The oldest of eight children, Marty and his family lived ten miles from the school, surrounded by farmland. Often, getting to LC required him to hop on his bike and make the journey to Lansdale so he could hit the weight room or play pickup basketball with classmates and friends from nearby North Penn and Methacton. His trip averaged sixteen or seventeen minutes, though his record time stands at thirteen when a summer thunderstorm chased him from the farmers' fields of his hometown of Harleysville to the three rolling fields of Lansdale Catholic.

I was an eighth grade student at Saint Stanislaus when one day it suddenly became abuzz with news from the high school just down the street. LC always dismissed earlier than the grade school, so the older students walking by would often give reports, if any, to teachers and students as they made their way home. On this day, they were excited that they had seen Dallas Cowboys star Tony Dorsett — giant rings, fancy fur coat, and all — walking the halls of their school. As a former player and alumnus of the University of Pittsburgh, he was there to recruit Marty to come play for the Panthers. (Several students reported that Dorsett commented about the students' school uniforms being green because they rooted for the Philadelphia Eagles.)

Marty wasn't a young man looking for a scholarship. He didn't have a Hudl account nor did he do most of the things that modern-day college recruiting prospects do today. What he did do was play with his God-given size, strength, and speed whether it was blocking an opponent on a football field, rebounding a basketball in the paint, or hurling a discus across the outskirts of a stadium track. He didn't even know that boys like him could get scholarships, thinking they were only meant for the skilled positions and the Tony Dorsetts of the world.

Before he graduated from Lansdale Catholic in June of 1981, Marty had at one point been one of the top ten discus throwers in the country, became the second boys basketball player to score over a thousand points, and led the Rare Breed to a tight-knit third place finish in what would be their final season in the Intercounty league against the teams of God's country. Joe Paterno from Penn State, Jackie Sherrill from Pitt and Gerry Faust, the newly hired coach at Notre Dame, all descended upon Lansdale Catholic. Their descent made Marty one of — if not *the* most highly recruited — players in the schools' history. By the time the recruiting visits from various coaches from three different sports were over, the unassuming young man known affectionately to the student body as "Jughead" (because his head was too big for the standard helmet) was on his way to play football for the University of Notre Dame, not even a mile away from where Big Jim had once studied to be a priest.

Size and scholarships would not become a Lansdale Catholic tradition, though grit and guts would. Tom Brown, the 5'4 wingback from the 1971 team; Jim Boaman, the three-time all-league nose tackle at 5'8 150 lbs.; and Donnie Drakas, a diminutive and powerful linebacker from the 1978 team, set the standard for the type of player that was formed and ultimately thrived at Lansdale Catholic. As the team moved into a brand new decade and sports league, the Bicentennial Athletic Conference, the success of the program remained heavily dependent on the average athlete who was willing to embrace the Rare Breed philosophy, push himself beyond mental and physical limitations, and approach each practice, off-season training session, and game with an unparalleled work ethic.

Of all the Algeo boys, for no one would this be truer than for Danny. Like our father, "Big" Jim, our second brother never grew over six feet like our other brothers would. His physical stature was opposite of that of the gargantuan Marty, and his personal demeanor was in fair contrast to that of older brother Jim, who was generally private and somewhat introverted. Whereas Jim would quietly disappear into his room in a state of seriousness to listen to Mick Jagger and gang in pre-game solitude, Dan was light and humorous, openly singing his favorite pop tunes of the day as if he had no cares or worries in the world. He frequently serenaded us with everything from Paul McCartney and the Wings to the Steve Miller Band to Frank Sinatra to Kate Smith.

In fact, many days in our childhood included hearing Kate Smith's roaring rendition of "God Bless America" belted out over the radio airwaves coming from Danny's room, where he learned the words. Growing up, my bedroom with my sisters was next to his for many years, and, from the time we were all very young, we would often hear the radio broadcasts of Philadelphia sporting events — Flyers, Sixers, Phillies, and Merrill Reese delivering the Eagles' commentary even when the game was on the family living room television. Danny lived, breathed, slept, and dreamt Philadelphia sports.

His love of sports, especially football, was immeasurable. On his bedroom wall were the annual team photographs from every Philly sports organization, tacked and slapped with brown masking tape on gaudy seventies wallpaper. However, as intense as his dedication to these professional teams was, his devotion to Rare Breed football was unparalleled. From the beginning, he was by Dad's side standing outside the huddle as the water and ball boy on the field. On Sunday evenings, when Big Jim rolled down the dining room shade after dinner to cast black and white game film from his 8 millimeter projector, Danny — and Veronica — would pull up a chair beside him. He was part of the Green and Gold team well before wearing a jersey. Former players and coaches were amazed at his encyclopedic memory and would often wonder how Dan could remember specific games, names, and plays that occurred when he would have been a young child. He was internet, before there was internet, when it came to storage of all things Lansdale Catholic Football.

As a child, I rarely saw Dan outside of school without a football in his hands. One time, in our West Ward backyard, I was about seven and doing cartwheels and handstands as he, about nine and proudly wearing his weathered Stanley Cup Flyers tee, tossed and kicked a football around. He suddenly stopped and asked me, "Do you think there is football in heaven?" Before I could answer, he promptly answered the question himself. "There's gotta be. There's just GOTTA be." Then he ran off, throwing the ball to himself, satisfied with his own conclusion.

A few years later, on a typical school morning, Mom sent me upstairs to Dan's room on the third floor to wake him. Normally, he and I were up early, devouring our bowls of cereal before the rest of the clan awoke. It seemed strange to all of us that he wasn't up for school yet, but we all just assumed that perhaps he had just overslept or maybe wasn't feeling well. It turned out to be neither. He wasn't in his room.

I was ten years old, and I couldn't believe how unusually calm my Mom was about *a missing child*. She dropped us all off at school as if her son had not suddenly disappeared that morning! I went through the day with nothing else on my mind except the fact that Dan was now a missing person. Finally, at the lunch table, I reported to my dining mates that my brother was gone, and we had no idea where he was.

I distinctly remember telling our lunch mother, who, in response to my story, repeatedly kept saying, "There has *got* to be some explanation," in her sweet Irish brogue.

When I got home, the first thing I did was ask if Danny was found.

"Yes, he is upstairs sleeping," Mickey replied casually as she stood at the stove preparing our *Waltons*-style nightly dinner. "He's been there all day."

"He wasn't there this morning," I replied.

"He was. You just didn't see him."

"What! No, I checked two times this morning. He wasn't there!"

She insisted he was and that somehow I missed him.

And she was half right. I *did* miss him because he wasn't there. Instead, he got up before the rest of the family, hopped the train to Philadelphia, and went out to go find Phillies home run king Mike Schmidt to offer to be his bat boy.

When he got off the train, though, he must have been overwhelmed by the city. He found the nearest phone booth and called home. Mom told him to stay put, then phoned a friend who had Philly connections, and by the afternoon, his mission to be a professional Philadelphia Phillies bat boy was abandoned, and Danny was back home and asleep in his bed by the time the rest of us returned from school that day.

I never knew any of this until thirty years later.

In that time, Danny never did become Mike Schmidt's bat boy, but that didn't stop him from dreaming other dreams and trying to make those dreams happen. As I said before, he was one sibling who understood how easily I got lost in my own dream world as our family drove to family parties and beach vacations and far away football games. If Dan had a vision, he was going to do everything he possibly could to make it a reality — and nothing was going to stop him.

*

One of the best loved football movies of all-time is set on the lovely autumn campus of Notre Dame University in South Bend, Indiana. I can't decide if this one is my favorite football movie or not, but I can tell you for sure that it is a top family hit with its historic setting, beautiful soundtrack and highly motivational storyline.

If you haven't seen this classic — or if you haven't seen it recently — it's always a film to watch every so often. It came out in 1993, a year before my son was born, and, when I watched it with him for the first time twenty years later, it was every bit as moving as the first time I saw it.

In its opening scene, *Rudy*, a diminutive but determined football player, is seen at his final high school practice. He is clearly unhappy that his career is over. Not only is his small size a factor, but he isn't particularly academic, which means that college is very unlikely and he will end up staying in his hometown in Ohio working in his father's factory.

But Rudy has another plan, much to the negative reaction of his family and fiancée, who ridiculed the notion that he could ever be accepted into the University of Notre Dame, let alone play for the world-renowned Fighting Irish. Besides his own mind and heart, the only person who believes in him is his best friend, Pete.

One of the most moving scenes in the movie is when, while on their lunch break, Pete remembers it's Rudy's birthday and unceremoniously presents him with a second-hand Notre Dame jacket wrapped in a grocery bag. Rudy realizes that his friend is the only one who believes in his dream.

I won't say too much about where the story goes after that, but I will say that, not long after, as Rudy is shaken by tragedy, he must face his own mortality and what he feels is a responsibility to his dream. He leaves his family, friends, and fiancée with what little money he has saved and heads to South Bend. He enrolls in Holy Cross, the college next door, what was once the seminary where Big Jim studied, on a mission to achieve the academic scores needed to be admitted to Notre Dame University.

Small in size, but big on dreams. This is a story my brother knew well.

Before Martin Roddy, Jr. walked across the ND campus in his size seventeen shoes, the worlds of massive Marty, the senior Fighting Irish recruit, and substantially shorter Dan Algeo, the sophomore son of the former Holy Cross seminarian, collided in the summer camp of 1980. For Danny and much of the Rare Breed, an encounter with Marty was like the "Tryouts" scene from Rudy, which can only be described as an intense battering session through which the physically smaller athlete battles almost completely on heart. Dan, with his history of going after dreams, embodied the Rare Breed player who may have been small, but went for big.

No matter how much staunchness they put out, the season following Marty's graduation was a rugged transition into the Bicentennial Athletic Conference, a conference consisting of schools from Bucks and Montgomery Counties considerably closer to Lansdale. For the next few years, the Rare Breed would face competitors from nearby area high schools in Jenkintown, New Hope, Springfield, Christopher Dock, Bristol, Morrisville, and Conshohocken.

Dan was a junior that first year in the new league, and, in spite of his team moving into the final game of the season without a single victory, the squad took their cue from players from previous seasons who were down on their luck when it came to posting in the "W" column. They didn't give up.

If there was something to salvage in that 1981 season, it was that we wouldn't go winless. It would have been the only winless season in league play if not for a single victory in the last game. For a season that had been particularly rough, I remember the ride home from Bristol was especially joyous. We were happy to get that one win. For now. A losing season would not become part of the Rare Breed tradition.

As Danny headed into his final year at LC, he hit the off-season hard. That summer, among our favorite outings as a family were seven-on-seven football contests in which he and the Rare Breed went against local teams. They were exciting games, but without pads, helmets, and the all-out intensity of autumn play. It didn't involve contact, as, instead of tackle, players ripped flags off the offensive opponent with the ball to stop the play.

It seemed like the safest possible way to play football, with hardly a risk of injury.

But Dan found a way to sprain his wrist one night. He fell on it hard and, much to his dismay, had to come out of the game for the rest of the evening. He iced it, rested it a few days, and then continued his summer training as usual.

When we went down the shore that August, I remember him packing his weights into a vehicle that was already carting over ten bodies, all our duffel bags, beach buckets, towels, sheets, and anything we could squeeze into that year's car to take to Sea Isle. But, along with his teammates, he was determined to make the season of 1982 a winning one, and was willing to do whatever he could to make himself the best player he could be.

I myself packed a basketball to bring to the shore city's popular outdoor court on John F. Kennedy Boulevard that welcomes visitors as they come across the bridge. But mostly, I made sure I had what every high school sophomore-to-be should have in her travel bag, according to teen beauty experts: shampoo, conditioner, face wash, astringent, sun lotion, foundation, pressed powder, lip gloss, and depilatory. I am sure I am missing a few items.

One day during an annual stay in Sea Isle, Danny took his weights alongside the pink house where there was an open space of grass where none of the younger kids could be found playing, and he began lifting weights and running sprints up and down Central Avenue. After about an hour, he came into the house, red-faced and sweaty, and proceeded to head to the shower.

The rest of us, having been at the beach for the day, were already showered and just hanging in the living room — which now had a television on which to watch *Friday Night Videos* — as we waited for dinner. Danny emerged from the bathroom with wet hair and pink legs. Not pink-skinned as some of us were, but pink with lotion.

"What do you have on your legs, Dan?" I asked.

"It's one of your lotions," he replied.

"Which one?" I responded.

"The one that says for your legs," he answered. "I needed something for my sore legs."

"That lotion is not for sore legs," I told him. "That's Nair!"

"What's Nair?"

"It's hair remover!"

With that, Dan launched one last sprint for the day down the hallway to wash the lotion off before it washed all his leg hair off.

Undaunted and with hair still remaining on his legs, he continued his training during our family vacation in New Jersey. Within two weeks, he knew that it would no longer be the off-season, but game time. As always, August football camp would be right there to greet us.

When we returned from Sea Isle that summer, Mickey discovered that Danny's July summer league injury had not healed. As she stood at the stove cooking for the Algeo masses one evening, Dan came in from camp.

"Look, I can do this with this hand," he said, vigorously shaking his left hand at the wrist. "But I can't do it to this one."

He tried to shake his right hand, but he could not without pain.

I was sixteen years old when I first heard of the word, "navicular". It is a very small bone in the wrist, and, when Danny had fallen and "sprained" his wrist, he had really fractured this bone. It required surgery, followed by a cast that would likely span the entirety of his senior year season.

I was also sixteen years old the first time I saw Big Jim cry.

The first few days of camp for Dad were long and intense, and, when he would come home that first week every year, the brutality of it was evident in his red burnt skin, sweaty hair, and hoarse voice. It was the routine. He was used to it, and so were we.

But this particular evening, he came home knowing Mom had the diagnosis from Dan's appointment with the doctor, and he went straight to the kitchen to hear it. I was sitting in the dining room with a clear view of them only feet away. There was a soft exchange between them. I didn't hear what Mick said to him. I only saw him look at her for a moment. Suddenly his face broke into such sadness that I can't put into words and an expression I had never seen on my father's face.

All I could hear him say was, "He worked so hard." Then he buried his face on my mom's shoulder. Heartbrokenness consumed our home for the next few days. Everyone was sad that Danny's senior year football season was over even before it had begun, as he truly lived and breathed LC football all three hundred and sixty-five days of the year.

Everyone, that is, except Dan.

*

In 1982, the average cost of gas was 91 cents per gallon, a United States postage stamp was 20 cents, the price of a new home went for $82,000, and buying a new car (which we didn't) would have cost about $7,983.00. *Knight Rider*, *Magnum PI*, and *Hill Street Blues* were popular TV shows, while *E.T.*, *Rocky III*, and *Poltergeist* were hits at the box office. We were still listening to vinyl and cassettes even as the first CD player was sold in Japan, and Michael Jackson thrilled the world with, at over 66 million copies sold, the best-selling album ever.

In Lansdale, Big Jim and his band of assistants were pushing, strategizing, training, instructing, and preparing Green and Gold football for their second season in the Bicentennial Athletic League. Assistant Anthony Sandone, Sr. was now joined by Doug Grunklee, Earl Alcott, Dick Zeigler, and John Davis. After a dismal debut that ended on a high note with a victory in Bristol, they were looking to carry the momentum into the fall of 1982.

Alongside Dan, who was now sidelined with a cast from his wrist almost all the way up his arm to his elbow, was his best friend and almost-clone Daniel Collins, who represented the last in the line of the Collins and Wisniewski families that played since the birth of the Rare Breed.

Dan and Dan were part of an eighteen-senior team, featuring the offensive dynamic duo of Thomas Lewandowski and Christopher Henderson, as well as the passing threat of the tall and long Bob DiPasquale. Anthony Picozzi, Dave Steglik, Jim Bagnell, and Bobby Williamson packed power and muscle to round out the team's leadership. With a strong underclass contingent, including Anthony Sandone, Jr., Pat Nolan, Mike Hino, and Steve of the Roddy Clan, a Bicentennial Athletic League Championship was well within reach.

The single BAL powerhouse dominating the league on the football field were the Saints of Archbishop Kennedy High School in Conshohocken. Once known as Saint Matthew's Parish High School, Archbishop Kennedy, under the prowess and direction of coaching pioneer Chris Bockrath, reversed a three-season winning drought in the mid-seventies to become one of the most successful football programs in the area of the late seventies and eighties. The late Bockrath, who many saw as a coach ahead of his time, went 124-82-6 in 21 years at Kennedy, collecting thirteen league titles along the way. His squad of perennial favorites would be the Rare Breed's biggest challenge.

The Green and Gold of Lansdale Catholic rebounded from their single-win season with a nearly perfect record in league play, managing to beat every team but the Saints. For Danny, the victories of his final season at Lansdale Catholic were moral. His injury healed enough for John Davis, the team trainer, to create a soft cast which allowed him to play again. In doing so, he and his classmates positioned LC to be within striking distance of Archbishop Kennedy, who hoarded the championship crown for yet another year.

Dan's very last game as a player for Big Jim took place right in Lansdale at North Penn High School, where the crosstown rival matchup resumed every Thanksgiving morning beginning in 1981. The tradition evolved into a community event that included a breakfast for the players and a 10 AM coin toss. Our aunts, uncles, and cousins would often start their day at Crawford Stadium with us, our Uncle Jim bringing three dozen donuts as our own pre-game meal.

Before the game began, the official approached the sideline to inform Dad and the coaches that, for whatever reason, Dan would not be permitted to play with that particular cast. He had been allowed in previous games, but now, it appeared that Danny would not play in the final game of his football career. Mr. Davis, however, raced to come up with some contraption from the trainer's kit to protect his wrist and arm that seemed to satisfy the referees. Dan represented the number ten green and gold jersey one last time in a tight, low-scoring battle that went to the Knights, 6 to 14.

Seven months later, with giant fans humming in a hot and humid Lansdale Catholic gymnasium where our family took up one whole row of metal folding chairs, Danny received the school's Most Courageous Male Athlete Award for his demeanor when faced with what might have been a career-ending injury. It was a proud and tearful moment to watch him head up the wooden steps to the LC stage to receive his award. Things had not gone his way always, but he had made the best of it and was moving on.

Or so we thought. Danny did not move on from Rare Breed football for years to come. The very next year, when I was a junior, he joined Dad's coaching staff as the freshman football coach alongside Anthony Sandone, Sr.

Dan was often at Lansdale Catholic, almost as much as he had been as a student. One time, he arrived for practice in what my sisters and I called his "banana suit", a bright yellow sweatshirt with matching sweatpants. On our drive home from school that day, Big Jim lamented not knowing how to tell Dan that he was required to come to the school in attire that was different from his playing days. He needed a more professional, adult look now that he was no longer a student and a player.

My sisters and I were on it. We agreed that on any gift-giving occasion, such as his birthday or Christmas, we would buy new clothes to help renovate his wardrobe. If we were going shopping for new clothes at any time, we would invite him and help him select items that would be appropriate for the assistant coach that he now was for the Rare Breed program. We were on a mission, and Dan was our project.

Of course, he saw through our plan almost immediately, jokingly asking, "Are you trying to make me over?" We leveled with him, and from that point on, you would see him in a shirt and tie on the sidelines for games and respectable coaching gear for practices and scrimmages. We never saw the banana suit again.

Dan was on the sideline in the fall of 1983, when the Rare Breed was unable to even score against Archbishop Kennedy in a 28 to 0 rout. In fact, the Green and Gold also fell to the Springfield Spartans, another one of the Bicentennial League's yearly competitive programs. I remember Dad being particularly upset that year because he truly believed that his players had the ability to beat both these teams. In the meantime, the BAL Crown continued to elude his Lansdale Catholic football team.

Mickey was upset, too. During those years against the Bicentennial League teams of Montgomery and Bucks Counties, Mom took on a very new and different role. As the eighties began, Mickey decided one way to increase our family income was to drive the Saint Stanislaus School bus. She added driving the LC sports teams to her duties, and, when Anthony Sandone was a junior, he distinctly recalled that she wasn't happy when the players loaded her bus chatting after their loss.

"There were certain players that were laughing and having a good time, and she got on the bus and let them know that she wasn't happy. That bus went silent in seconds. And I thought it was great that she did that."

Dad and Mom clearly believed that the Rare Breed could beat Archbishop Kennedy and win the league title — and nobody should be happy about it until they did.

The players believed it, too, but, heading into the 1984 season, the local papers once again chose the Saints to win the league championship outright. It was my senior year, and my classmates were having one amazing season throughout September and October. Offensively, Anthony, Doug Perry, and Michael Totaro were putting points on the board while the defense, led by Steve Roddy, Jeff Kratz, and CB West transfer Steve Conduit, held its league opponents scoreless. On the first Friday night of November, under the lights of the Conshohocken A-Field, they would face the hands-down favorite, the Archbishop Kennedy Saints.

Along with Veronica, who did most of the calculations, I was the team statistician. The night of the game, I put in a few hours at my job, leaving early to find my way to Conshohocken from Lansdale without the benefit of a GPS, map, or cell phone to call someone for directions. Mickey had written down the way to the game on a piece of memo pad paper, which got me to the sideline as the first quarter ended. There were so many in attendance for one of the most hyped-up games that season that I sprinted to the field from where I had parked that year's used family car. It seemed like a mile away in the sea of vehicles filling the streets of Conshy that night.

What we watched was one of the most memorable and mysterious games in the area of that era. The Rare Breed, down at the half, played their hearts out on both ends of the ball, battling back to take a 22-14 lead with about a minute and a half to go. Suddenly, the scoreboard clock went dead, and the officials announced they would be keeping time on the field. I never knew ninety seconds to be as painfully long as it was that night, and, in that time, the Saints managed to score 8 more points to tie the game at 22-22 on an incredible reception by the talented Jimmy Borkowski. They also regained the ball and were marching down the field as the unseen time was ticking off the clock. One of my classmates, Jeff Kratz, made an amazing defensive play that caused the AK quarterback to cough up the ball, giving the Rare Breed possession and a chance to get on the board one more time in an effort to win the title undisputedly. As Lansdale Catholic recovered the fumble, the whistle blew to end the game.

In what the *Philadelphia Inquirer* deemed the high school athletic contest of the year, the Rare Breed of 1984 gained a share of the Bicentennial Athletic League Championship with the favored Archbishop Kennedy Saints. As the final whistle blew, the boys in blue and white cheered wildly as the boys in the green and gold were somber and silent. The tie did not sit well with our players. The next morning, we sat in the classroom at North Penn taking our SATs. I can still see the long and disappointed faces of my fellow classmates. They were wiped out. More than that, they felt that the tie was more like a loss, and they were not satisfied because they were capable of being the sole champions.

To this day, almost every LC player and coach can talk about that game as if it happened last night, so intense was the battle. That season's junior class felt the sting of the outcome all off-season long, and, in the fall of 1985, before exiting the Bicentennial League to join the then newly-formed Pioneer Athletic Conference the following season, the Rare Breed of Lansdale won the undisputed championship. Led by Michael Greer, Steve Adams, Remo DiFranceso (a senior who would have an unbelievable 18 tackles against Quakertown as a defensive tackle), Christopher (the last of the six Walsh brothers), and Michael (the youngest) Wagner, a determined cast of Crusaders beat every single league opponent, including Archbishop Kennedy in a decisive 28-6 victory, before moving on.

The PAC-8, which would later become the PAC-10, debuted its first season in the fall of 1986. Lansdale Catholic joined seven other teams from Montgomery County: Springford, Upper Perkiomen, Perkiomen Valley, Pottsgrove, Pottstown, Phoenixville, and Saint Pius X.

Brother Jim, who had briefly coached with Dad while on a break from college in 1981, was now again on the Rare Breed sidelines. He would be part of the coaching contingent there for three years from for the first PAC-10 season, departing after the 1988 season to become a steady presence on the coaching staff with league opposition, Pottsgrove.

The Rare Breed launched a rocky start in their competitive new conference. They would not earn a single league crown as they navigated through the last few years of the eighties. But they had been here before, somewhere in the middle of the pack in standings, where they had to figure out this new cast of opponents and strengthen their program to outplay them.

Big Jim, one of the founding members of the PAC-10, continued the Thanksgiving tradition with North Penn through the eighties. He and the players loved having a shot at upsetting one of the biggest schools in the state each holiday. The boys between the teams were usually friends, having grown up together around the neighborhoods of Lansdale. The Knights would almost always prevail, though the scores were hardly lopsided and the games were most definitely battles.

In the mid-eighties, WNPV, our local radio station, would hire a new sports director in Rick Woelfel, who became one of the most prominent area sports writers for a variety of local newspapers, including several Montgomery County publications, *The Intelligencer*, and *The Bucks County Courier Times*. He recalled his first experience with the Thanksgiving game and the Rare Breed Spirit.

"I first encountered Coach Algeo in the fall of 1985, a few months after being hired as the sports director at WNPV radio. At the time, Lansdale Catholic played its home games on Saturday nights at what later became Crawford Stadium at North Penn. Calling those games, often with LC grad John Wagner in the booth with me, brings back some wonderful memories.

"That first season my dad was losing his battle with cancer. Every time I would see Coach Algeo, or Mrs. Algeo, they would ask how he was doing. That is something I'll never forget. That Thanksgiving I had the privilege of calling my first North Penn-Lansdale Catholic game, which became one of my favorite events of the year to cover. It was postponed on Thanksgiving morning because of snow and played two days later on Saturday.

"My dad was listening on the radio. I remember saying to John before we took the air that this game, a 7-6 LC win, was likely the last football game my dad would hear me broadcast. That turned to be the case, he passed away the following February.

"From the start, it was obvious how much Coach Algeo cared about his family and the young men who played for him. He was extraordinarily supportive and protective of both and much like my own father in that regard. And his faith was and is extremely important to him. Working with Coach Algeo for some three decades, first as a broadcaster, then as a writer, was always a pleasure. He understood, as much as any coach I've ever worked with, the axiom that high school sports are intended to be a teaching ground and extension of the classroom and that he was preparing his student-athletes for manhood. It is difficult to imagine anyone having a better or more caring guide and mentor."

With that mentorship nearing twenty years, in the fall of 1986, Mr. Woelfel witnessed M.J. Grourke, Bob Culp, and Ray Liberto lead the Rare Breed squad as they edged out the growing Pennsylvania football powerhouse across town, 7 to 6. Two years later, in one of the most memorable Thanksgiving contests that decade, the Rare Breed delighted the LC fans with a 25-0 triumph. A spunky young quarterback, Noell Maerz, and fierce ensemble that included Mark McKnutt, Chris Malatesta, and Michael Kuhn slipped and slid their way to a muddy victory on a balmy November morning.

These rare wins always made the Thanksgiving dinner just a little more festive. There is nothing worse than a game you believed you could have won, and Dad and his budding body of vocal family sports analysts felt that way about a lot of the Turkey Day match-ups. The win-loss record accumulated over the years did not truly reflect the intensity of those late autumn clashes in front of fervent Lansdale crowds.

Thanksgiving, regardless, was always a family holiday favorite, and a tough loss in a close game often only accentuated the truly important stuff of life. After a day of football, parades, donuts, every Thanksgiving dish and pie that could possibly be put on one table, and evening family pickup games on the LC basketball court, Big Jim always gave the toast — football was good, but strong faith and the good health and blessing of his family are what mattered.

Still, the best combination remained embodied in the three fields' mantra of "Faith, Family, and Football," and as another decade of Rare Breed football was coming to an end, a lot of changes were happening besides the graying of Big Jim's once black head of curls. It was now over twenty years since Big Jim's first game, and so much had changed since the first time Father O'Donnell and Paul Jefferies offered Dad the position of head football coach at Lansdale Catholic.

Dan, although steady as an assistant varsity coach for the better part of the eighties, started to ripen as a young man as the nineties approached. He began taking college courses on his path to become a teacher and, along with his sidekick Dan Collins, helped pioneer the men's basketball program at Gwynedd Mercy University. Coach Sandone and he continued to develop the boys coming in as freshmen to the LC football program, many of them never having played the sport a day in their lives. It was not without some challenges, such as when Danny mistakenly scheduled the freshmen squad to play a renowned school for juvenile delinquents. Apparently, this was known to everyone but him, and his fourteen-old players just learning the game found themselves on the line of scrimmage facing eighteen year-olds with muscles, mustaches, and, yes, that thing called size. Dan kept learning, though, with the dream that he would become a head coach one day.

Also on the Green and Gold sidelines were Mary Eileen and Mary Frances, who had inherited the statistician positions handed down by the older sisters, and John Patrick, now the eleven-year old playing touch football with a score of other kids behind the stands. Veronica had become part of the coaching staff, communicating via headsets with the assistants as she was perched atop the press box for an aerial view of the game. Jim married Mary Wilson with a new coaching position and their first child on the way. Mary Beth was preparing to wed Scott Dewey. Maggie and Mike now had two children, Michael and Jackie. I had graduated from Lansdale Catholic and, alongside Veronica, learned to play lacrosse at Ursinus College, where our team won the Division III National Championship in my senior year.

That same year, my LC classmate, Steve Roddy (brother of the sizeable Marty) played for Coach Lou Holtz and won the National Championship as part of the Notre Dame Fighting Irish. The champions were invited to Washington, DC. Steve and his teammates were photographed with President Ronald Reagan in his final days as leader of the free world in 1989. That year not only brought the end of the Reagan era, which had spanned almost the entire decade, but it also gave us the *Batman* movie starring Michael Keaton and Prince's rocking musical rendition of the same name. Madonna, Paula Abdul, Janet Jackson, and Milli Vanilli all topped the music charts. Gas was averaging 97 cents a gallon, a new home was $120,000, a new car $15,350, and the cost of a US postage stamp was now 25 cents. Pope John Paul II, in his eleventh year of the papacy, remained head of the Roman Catholic Church.

In Pennsylvania, the high school football landscape was drastically changing, as just months before, in the fall of 1988, the Pennsylvania Interscholastic Athletic Association introduced its first ever state play-off system. Now, on each side of the Keystone State, the best of the league would play the best of the district, and the best of the district would play the best in the state. The entire journey would end in an East-West showdown at Hershey Stadium in Hershey, Pennsylvania.

To the rest of the world, Hershey is known as Chocolate Town, USA. Just fourteen miles east of the state capitol of Harrisburg, it is named after Milton Snavely Hershey, the American confectioner and philanthropist who gave the world Hershey bars, kisses, candy, and Hersheypark. Milton's own life is a story in itself, as at the Hershey School in his hometown, there is a bronze statue of him holding a parentless boy in his arms. He took care of people — his family, his employees, their children, and orphans.

Milton Hershey inspired many people in several ways. He had traveled to Chicago, New York, and Philadelphia to establish his candy business, only to return having failed. He persevered, ultimately using the cow milk from farmland surrounding him his whole life to build his successful, worldwide company. Along with that, he opened a famous amusement park built initially for the children of his employees, as well as a school for orphans that still serves two thousands students today. I am pretty certain, however, he had no idea in the early part of the twentieth century just how much the name Hershey would inspire young high school football players across Pennsylvania to dream of a season at the end of which they and their team would be deemed the best in the entire state there.

At just eleven years old then, our youngest brother, John Patrick, was still walking the halls of the grade school across the street from our big and beautiful Saint Stanislaus Church. But one day soon, he would be one of those dreamers.

CHAPTER SIX

Sons of the Nineties

*For momentary, light affliction is producing for us an
eternal weight of glory far beyond all comparison.*

~ 2 Corinthians 4:17

From the ceremonious day that John Patrick was born, he literally grew up
with brothers and sisters who were MVPs, Top Ten scholars, and scholarship athletes. He was surrounded by trophies, titles, and championships
of all kinds from all different sports. He started attending sporting events
basically right from the crib. He witnessed coaches' meetings, training
sessions, game film, scouting, and a great deal of successes in the pursuit
of athletic excellence. From an early age, he was immersed in the work
ethic that we lived in our home and was carried daily the two miles to
Lansdale Catholic.

In Dan's final year of high school at LC, he often drove Veronica and
me home from basketball practice. On this one particular early evening,
as the three of us pulled up along the curve in our creaky Gran Torino, we
saw John sprinting the length of the sidewalk to the corner, about 50 yards,
and back.

"What are you doing, John?" one of us asked him.

"I am working on my form," he replied.

"Your form?" asked Dan.

"My running form," answered John.

He was five.

By that time, our family life not only consisted of almost everybody playing sports, but the "normal" thing of watching movies on cable as well. The number of television options in our household was now respectable. Gone were the days when I had to make a case for my film choice to be on the living room set or be forced to slip away to my parents' room to watch a movie that did not achieve a consensus vote.

Increasing the number of television sets in our home was one thing, but getting cable into the Algeo house was, at first, quite a challenge. We had convinced Big Jim to pay a monthly cable bill, but only when he learned there was a 24-hour all sports network. He discovered something called ESPN, and we got to watch countless showings of *Mr. Mom*, *Sixteen Candles*, and *Yentl*. It was a win-win.

One afternoon, we came home from school and turned on *Yentl* for what was probably the fifteenth or sixteenth time. If you do not know the story of Yentl, it is a film made by Barbra Streisand. She produced, directed, acted, and sang every word about a Jewish girl alone in the world who craves to learn. When her papa dies, she cuts her hair and disguises herself as a boy so that she can study the Torah.

At one point in the movie, as all the young men take a breather from their studies, they strip down to swim in a nearby lake. The scholars try to convince Yentl to join them, but, for obvious reasons, she cannot. It is truly an innocent and comical scene, harmlessly showing the backsides of the male students entering the water as Yentl tries to hide her face in a book at the sight.

It is also the scene that Big Jim happened to come home to following an afternoon on the practice field. To our eyes was a funny sequence where a young woman disguised as a boy is trying to avoid their buck naked swim. To his eyes was a room full of children watching naked men on his living room television set. To him, it looked like his kids were enjoying nude movies.

When he saw the scenario, he froze, door still halfway open behind him. We all froze, too, even though we were guilty of nothing. He demanded that we change the channel.

Great.

None of us even bothered to try to explain, and one of us got up and turned the channel, probably to ESPN, as he made his way into the kitchen to greet Mom. Sometimes, I guess it's just easier to not present a defense and let time have its way with these sorts of things. The whole episode was completely forgotten anyway, when not long afterwards, ESPN broadcast a more pleasing movie that became a household favorite, and particularly for our youngest brother John.

If you ask most people about a Notre Dame Football movie, I think they'd be likely to say *Rudy* or, possibly, *Knute Rockne All-American*. But at 526 Columbia Avenue, the most watched Notre Dame movie of all time was a documentary we first saw on the Entertainment and Sports Programming Network, and it was called *Wake Up The Echoes*.

In it, the legendary John Facenda narrates the unique and storied history of Notre Dame Football, from Knute Rockne to Frank Leahy to Ara Parseghian to Lou Holtz. John Patrick watched it so much, the tape on the video cassette got completely worn out that it was ultimately no longer viewable after a few years. It did not stop us from enjoying the many Fighting Irish players recount entertaining stories and poignant moments so often that we knew most of the tales and quotes by heart.

Perhaps one of the most quoted in our family was by John Lattner, a two-time Maxwell Club Award and Heisman Trophy winner in the early fifties. As a halfback for Coach Frank Leahy, the highly successful head coach would often joke with the confident young freshman, with his strong Irish brogue, that he was a "cruiser." When John Patrick strolled onto the Lansdale Catholic campus in 1992, my sisters and I changed his quote just a little bit — but keeping the Irish brogue — to suit our youngest brother, poised to stroll the halls of LC.

The nineties had cruised in with its curtained hair, high waisted jeans, and colorful turtlenecks. By 1993, Bill Clinton succeeded George Bush as President of the United States, apartheid ended in South Africa after three years of negotiations, and Michael Jordan was leading the Chicago Bulls to another NBA World Championship. The price of gas was now over a dollar at $1.16 per gallon, the cost of a postage stamp climbed to 29 cents, and dinosaurs dominated movie theaters as Mariah Carey, Garth Brooks, and Nirvana crooned over the airwaves.

It was not the first time our family experienced death, but it came to break our hearts hard nonetheless with passing of our grandmothers, just months apart. Pop Filliben had passed away a year after I was born, and Pop-pop Algeo when I was away volunteer teaching in New Orleans in 1990, immediately following college graduation. There was something comforting in still having our Nanny and Nana with us. But, by the fall of 1993, God called them Home, too.

The loss of all our grandparents was not something I was nor any of us were prepared for. The day that the Reese Street house was sold was eye-opening for me. Our family had sung and danced and celebrated there so many times. I couldn't believe we would never step foot in that place of joyful memories ever again, that those days there were gone forever. The festive table, the sound of song, the strumming of the guitar, and a roomful of children inventing dance moves across its rug — these moments there would now only be recollected on small film clips stored in my heart. The unexpected void heightened my sense of family at a time when I, carrying my son, was beginning my own.

Jim and Mick's expanding clan of grandchildren had now reached four, with mine and Mary Frances' on the way. Jimmy and Mary's first daughter, Shannon, was born. Mary Beth and Scott welcomed their daughter Maeve. Maggie and Mike had moved into the Lansdale area with Jackie and Mike, who was two years behind his Uncle John. It would not be long before John and Mike would be part of the Rare Breed tradition.

Until then, the PAC-10 wasn't as easy to crack as the previous two leagues. Multiple area teams vied for the top position in hotly contested competitions each season. In almost ten years, between 1986 and 1995, four different teams won the championship, with the Rams of Spring-Ford High School earning half of them. Lansdale Catholic got as close to the title as second place and as far from it as fourth in nearly a decade of conference play.

Still, not only did teams know that the Rare Breed could not be taken for granted, but individual performers continued to emerge from the program. With Class of 88 Michael Chermela becoming the first player to run 1,000 yards, the list of dominant LC players lengthened as the 1980s rolled into the 1990s. Billy Knapp. George Haldeman. Bill Doughty. Chris Bair. Dave Delciotto. Jason Chermela. Michael Chermela. Erich Maerz. Patrick Roddy. Joe McAteer. Joe Trave. Rob McMaster.

Before long, John Algeo, tall and lean and standing at 6 feet 2 inches, would find his place among the honor roll call of these celebrated Lansdale Catholic players.

On October 23, 1993, John Patrick, now a sophomore, cracked the starting lineup and never looked back. With the senior quarterback suffering an ankle injury from the previous week's contest, Big Jim made the decision to start John in a mid-season battle with Pottsgrove, as his brother Jim stood directly across from the Rare Breed sideline as an assistant for the opposition. At the sight of the #15 running out to lead the offense as the field general, big brother Jim sounded the alarm on the Falcons sideline.

"We're in trouble," he declared bluntly. And he was right.

With a 275-pound fullback in Greg Fitzsimmons and an athletic arsenal of talents the likes of John Woehlcke, Mike Bender, and Matt Bender, LC dominated the match-up, 29-6, and John secured his place as first-string quarterback from that day on. The team finished 5-5-2, but, more importantly, started gaining momentum as they barreled toward the fall of 1994. An intense enthusiasm was carried through the high school football cycle of off-season weight training, spring practice, summers of seven-on-seven, and the Algeo summer vacation.

When our glorious annual fortnight on the beaches of Sea Isle City came to end that August, freshman Michael deMarteleire, only two years younger than his Uncle John, arrived onto the LC campus and went straight to its three fields. He was one of the few freshmen ever to play Rare Breed varsity, with only a handful of first-year players reaching high school prime time. Big Jim also brought on Mike deMarteleire, Sr., Dan Shallow, and Michael "Wags" Wagner (brother to John) to join brother Dan assisting in the coaching duties on the sidelines.

The predictions for league success were mixed. Some preseason picks ranked the Rare Breed as low as ninth once all the conference competitors had a shot at each other. With John in his second year as quarterback and Michael "deMart" Jr. as one of his wide receivers, Lansdale Catholic managed a 6-3 record in the PAC-10, with the title of league champions continuing to elude them as they landed in third place behind regular contenders Spring-Ford and Phoenixville.

But now, since almost six hundred Pennsylvania teams were divided into four classes of play, they were able to chase another title once the conference position-elbowing had ended. Now, unlike Dad's earlier teams in the Intercounty League and Bicentennial Athletic Conference, there was a play-off season, and, in November 1994, the Lansdale Catholic Football won its first Class AA District Title, dominating Oxford 35-7.

The next game, they were officially in state playoffs, falling to Mount Carmel, 41 to 22, in their first ever appearance. The Red Tornadoes then roared on to win their first state crown. They would return to Hershey several more times to do so.

But as helmets and cleats were hung for another season, spirits at the corner of Seventh Street and Lansdale Avenue were flying high and expectations were big. Even though they largely competed against Class AAA and AAAA in the Pac-10, maybe next season would be their year to finally win the league title. Now that the Rare Breed had, for the first time, captured a District Crown and reached a state playoff game, visions of chocolate kisses were dancing in their heads.

And maybe, a trip to Hershey wasn't just a dream after all.

*

Dad's taste of PIAA state playoffs was tantalizing. To be on the path to a possible state crown is not easy in a crowd of almost six hundred teams.

"You can say it's just another game," he said of the Mount Carmel clash, "but it's different."

Having won the District Crown for the first time, there was a palpable excitement around John's senior year Rare Breed team, and more than one high school football enthusiast tossed the notion of a state championship into the preseason ring of predictions. What began as play and travel among battling teams confined to one or two counties on Dad's opening game night in 1968 was now blooming into a chance to possibly venture to places in Pennsylvania that were often unknown to these boys — and, better yet, come home with the State trophy.

But first, the season. We were well aware how preseason predictions could quickly blow up in smoke. Having lost offensive talents Rob McMaster and Scott Garner, the Rare Breed would be heavily dependent on this explosive trio of John, Sean Buchy, and Rob Carickhoff to ride them to a victorious season. John was coming off a 2,020 yard and 17-touchdown season as a junior, while Sean scored 13 times the previous year. The team would not be traveling anywhere, however, without its punishing defensive unit. Mike Oberholtzer, Mark Tavani, Joe Collella, Neil Greene, and Ryan McCarthy were that unit. In the wings, varsity newcomers Mike deMarteleire, Jr., Chris Walsh, and Joe Keating were all hungry to unleash their offensive force on the field.

As much as the fiery brew excited Big Jim and the entire coaching staff, Dad usually downplayed expectations. He never really did suggest to local reporters just how good he thought his team was. On this rare occasion, heading into football season 1995, he did express a hint of his hope that state playoffs were in the Rare Breed's future.

But, first, the so-far impenetrable PAC-10 Title. In conference play, as a small Class AA team, Lansdale Catholic continued to face imposing competition from the sizeable PAC-10 schools, who were mainly AAA and AAAA. Fueling on the confidence of its 1994 postseason success, the Rare Breed hoped to finally capture the league title.

A challenge could be expected in nearly every PAC-10 contest, and one obstacle to this achievement would be the Pottsgrove Falcons, where our brother Jim entered his seventh year of assistant coaching. The Lansdale Catholic Crusaders, with John quarterbacking both his sophomore and junior years, had bested the Falcons, both in his first QB start, 29 to 6, and the follow-up performance, 34 to 14.

But on this night, the Falcons were getting the best of the Crusaders. By halftime, Pottsgrove had put up 28 points, while LC could only muster a paltry 7. The dynamic Rare Breed offense had sputtered, and its powerful defense had no answers that night for the opposition. After two quarters, both teams left the field and disappeared into the locker rooms.

Funny thing about halftimes. In the world of high school football, there seems to be this unspoken code that what happens in the locker room stays in the locker room. No matter what is said, done, hollered, whispered, pleaded, or promised, we were never really given the details. Occasionally, though rarely, I might get a tidbit of information later from Danny if I asked, "What in the world happened at halftime?"

Fans on both sides of the stadium were asking the same question that night because the Rare Breed came out as if a brand new team and launched a reversal of performance on both ends of the football. John and the offense mounted a 22-point campaign in the second half, posting a total of 29 points on the board before the final whistle blew. The defense, for their part, thwarted every single offensive card the Falcons showed, allowing not one single point in the third and fourth quarters. The Rare Breed emerged with the victory, 29-28.

The amazing comeback was one of six league victories that season. They did not prove to be enough to capture the PAC-10 title, finishing with a 6 - 3 league record and in a tie for third place with Great Valley, behind Spring-Ford and Pottstown. They were enough, however, to set the Green and Gold on course to compete for the District I Championship.

And so Big Jim and Company went riding, as did all the Football Family, with our signs and cowbells and foam Number One fingers. For the second straight year, the Rare Breed won the District I AA Title, beating Springfield of Montgomery County, 28-6. The win put the team in state playoffs once again and positioned them for one of the best high school football games, in all our many journeys from stadium to stadium, I have ever witnessed.

It was also one of the most freezing cold game nights I will ever remember and took place the day after Thanksgiving. With the PIAA state playoff system now in place for eight years, there was no Turkey Day contest against the North Penn Knights, our big crosstown rival, that season. In fact, post-season success year after year for both squads would mean less and less of the hometown event.

On this Black Friday, I gathered my son Dillon, a few months past his first birthday, my godson Shane, who was a year older, and, Laura, my best friend since college, to make the hike from Bucks County, Pennsylvania to Plymouth Whitemarsh High School an hour away in Plymouth Meeting, PA. I joined the rest of our clan, most with families of their own now and coming from as far as Maryland, to watch what could be John Patrick's final game of his high school career. At this stage of the season, a loss meant the end.

On this brutal night, as the kids of the family were jammed into their winter snowsuits and shuffled in and out of our heated vehicles just within viewing distance of the stadium field, the Lansdale Catholic Crusaders and the Dunmore Bucks engaged in state playoff battle that would send one team home and one team a game closer to Hershey.

The Bucks of Dunmore hailed from up above Scranton in Northeastern PA, affectionately known as NEPA. The Bucks, coached by the legendary Jack Henzes, were bringing their own special tenacious brand of "God, Family, Dunmore Bucks" to the field that night. In fact, they took the lead and never looked back for most of the game.

The Rare Breed, down 14 to 12 late in the fourth quarter, launched an offensive surge after defensive end Mike Oberholtzer and the defensive squad came up huge with less than a minute to play. The offense returned the favor, as Rob Carickhoff's single catch of the night turned out to be a critical third down completion that put the Rare Breed inside the five-yard line. John, who had delivered a touchdown pass to Greg Kozminski in the first half just minutes before halftime, rushed into the end zone for the game-winning touchdown in the second half. The Rare Breed won 18 to 12 and was moving on.

The electricity in the air following Big Jim's deepest state playoff victory literally took the chill out of the stadium air for the Lansdale Catholic fans. Among them sat twenty-three-year-old Chris Mooney, who had just accepted the head coaching position for the boys' basketball team. Currently at the helm of the Richmond University program (where he just recorded his 250th win), Mooney was a graduate of Archbishop Ryan High School in Philadelphia and the runner-up for the Ivy League Rookie of the year as a four-year starter at Princeton. In 1995, fresh out of college, Mooney took the reins of the boys' hoops squad at Seventh Street and Lansdale Avenue.

Upon watching John's performance against the Bucks, he penned him a letter, asking him to play for the basketball team. It seems one play, in particular, left an impression on Mooney and many of the fans that night.

John had thrown a perfect pass right into the hands of one of his team-mates alone in the end zone as time was ticking off the clock. As happens, the pass was dropped. Without hesitation, John raced up to the player, who was clearly angry at his own mistake, and refused to let him get down. He had rallied his team with undaunted leadership and a rushing performance that earned him the nickname "Jogging John."

The decision to play basketball, a sport he had left four years before, had to wait. The Crusaders marched on to the next battle, where they beat Northern Lehigh, 20 to 6. The win put them in the distinguished field of being only one of four teams left alive in the state of Pennsylvania. One more win would give the Rare Breed a trip to Hershey. Two more wins would give them its first-ever state championship.

On a Friday in December of 1995, the Rare Breed Football Family followed the fifty-two man roster to Dauphin County, where Lansdale Catholic faced the formidable Bishop McDevitt. McDevitt, wearing blue and gold and also known as the Crusaders, entered the battle with a perfect 14-0 record and the District 3 Title.

As when Maggie's team made the Final Four some fifteen years before, I was unable to attend due to a school commitment. After work that evening, as I went shopping, I sat with toddlers Dillon and Shane in a parking lot on the Levittown Parkway in Bucks County, fiddling with a dated tuner in search of my hometown radio, 1440 AM, WNPV.

On the broadcast was former player and assistant coach, Joe Ritinski. Beside him was the legendary local personality, Mr. Jim Church. His being there was only fitting. Two years after Dad took hold of the reigns at LC, the voice of high school sports began calling the area football and basketball games. Since 1970, Mr. Church color commentated thousands of games and interviewed at least as many athletes and coaches on his Saturday morning show, *On The Bench*. With his sheer enthusiasm and ability to accentuate the positive, Mr. Church became cherished as a respected advocate of the high school athlete and what can be accomplished through sport.

In my white little 1989 vehicle, which was one hundred and six miles away from their press box, the voices of former Coach Ritinski and Mr. Church were faint and crackling as I strained to listen to the low-scoring contest. For almost an hour, my ear was inches away from the speaker, trying to determine who had possession, how much time was left, what down was it from my muddled connection with the station.

In the remaining moments, I was able to hear the final touchdown by the *other* Crusaders, to my dismay, just getting by with a 12-7 victory over the Rare Breed of Lansdale before they moved on to the Hershey title game the following week. There, they claimed the state crown in a 29-0 win over the Burrell Bucs of Westmoreland County.

As disappointed as Dad, John, and the Crusaders of Lansdale were, the Football Family who had made the ride to Dauphin County erupted with proud applause at the season the team had given itself and its fans. The taste of defeat was bitter, but there was no hanging of heads to be had. In less than a decade of the inception of the state championship, the Rare Breed had come just one game away.

I had learned once already that you can come so close to that state crown and never have another chance at it again. Rare Breed 1995 brought us within inches of the big coveted blue and gold state trophy, it was almost touchable. And when you come that close to something so prestigious, you don't forget the thrill, the excitement, and the pain of just missing getting your fingers around it. You long for the chance to get up and go for that moment of glory again.

That night saw the last of my brothers play football for Big Jim. As an elementary school child and teenage seminarian, he could not have known in his *Catholic Boy* magazine days the joy he would have coaching, in addition to the two thousand he would ultimately mentor, his own three sons. In June of 1996, he watched — and we along with him — his youngest cruise from the halls and fields of Lansdale Catholic and ride off to those of Cornell University just a few short months later.

But, before moving on, John did take Coach Mooney's invitation to play and start varsity basketball and placed third in the state in the track and field mile, even with a case of asthma. And while the second generation of Algeos in our Football Family had come to an end, a third generation had already begun.

*

The road to Hershey stopped one game shy of the coveted trip to claim the state crown, but we continued to ride once the season ended, even if it was only as far as school and Sunday Mass and our annual summer drive to Sea Isle City. The rides down the shore were different now. Those early days of somehow squeezing nine children with beach buckets and coolers and duffel bags into one station wagon were nearly extinct. Now, most of Big Jim and Mick's nine children were grown and raising families of their own.

It struck me by the end of the nineties, when my parents would call, telling me to come down the shore with Dillon, how they never seemed happier than when a son or daughter would bring their own children through the doors of the summer rental. Nothing made them happier than when they finally — after a year of a grueling schedule, scouting, clinics, offseason training, seven-on-sevens, and weight room sessions — were unpacked on the first day at the shore house. I will always remember to the day I die the look of joy and contentment as each of us arrived. Nanny Algeo's motto of "what's one more potato in the pot" was alive and well and growing bigger and merrier.

A typical day at the beach in the late nineties looked like a glimpse of heaven. The younger children would be digging their own pools into the Sea Isle sand, and the older ones would flit from paddle ball tournaments, wiffle ball games, and frisbee tosses. Mom and the other family readers situated themselves right along the water's edge in their long and low beach chairs. Big Jim could often be found floating on his back alone in the water, staring at the blue sky above, cherishing the few days of the year when he cleared his mind of football.

Not everybody, however, was taking a break from football. Young Michael, now the only family playing for the Rare Breed, and his friends created their own field in the sand, digging the sidelines and end zones by dragging their feet. Here, the play was just that. Play. They kept score at times, and yet other times, the boys just goofed off by designing dream plays with just seconds left.

They must have done something right down on the Sea Isle City beaches. In the fall of 1996, after ten years of the PAC-10 Conference escaping them, Michael deMarteleire and a talented cast of Rare Breed players won the league crown with a record of 8 wins and 1 loss. After a 14-7 win over Upper Merion in District playoffs, the team fell to AAA powerhouse Strath Haven, 41-20, thus ending young Mike's junior season. As 1997 and Michael's final season approached, Dad and the team set their sights on repeating the league championship, but, this time, aiming to add a District Title and a bid at Hershey.

In 1997, Big Jim was now 61 years old and still living his boyhood dream with Mickey, maintaining a very youthful 58. By this time, Danny had left the Rare Breed sidelines following John Patrick's final season. He met and married Courtney Fitzsimmons, the sister of five LC players, in March of 1996. It was an eventful time for the clan, as just days before the ceremony, the family welcomed Jonathan Traywick on the Feast of St. Joseph. Only hours before the wedding, Dan found out that he was named the head football coach of The Cahillites of Roman Catholic High School in Philadelphia.

The history of Roman Catholic was founded on a dream of a nineteenth-century merchant in Philadelphia. His vision was to create a school that offered a free Catholic education for boys after elementary school. Cahill died in August of 1978, but his dream did not pass with him. In 1890, the school affectionately known as "Roman" opened its doors. It was able to maintain free admission until increasing costs of staffing and facilities ended the policy in the 1960s.

Twenty-five years later, the Purple and Gold of Roman Catholic High School were on the chopping block due to low enrollment. In 1985, the Archdiocese slated the institution for closure, but the 70-year strong Alumni Association banded together, raising the necessary funds and increasing the school's enrollment. The dream of Thomas Cahill on the corner of Broad and Vine Streets lived on. Here, Danny's dream to become a head high school football coach came alive.

Danny already had a season with the Cahillites under his belt by the time Michael was a senior and 1997 had rolled in. The cost of gas was now $1.22 a gallon, a new house averaged $124,100, and a dozen eggs went for about $1.17. The world was shocked by the death of the "People's Princess", Diana. In song, Hanson brought an end to the grunge era with its light and happy "Mmmbop", and No Doubt burst onto the music scene with its *Live In The Tragic Kingdom* debut. Celine Dion belted the theme song to *Titanic*, the wildly popular Oscar winner that became the first film to break the billion-dollar mark.

That year, on the corner of Seventh Street and Lansdale Avenue, the Rare Breed returned to camp and barreled their way through the PAC-10, winning their second consecutive league title, along with co-champion Upper Perkiomen. Those same Upper Perkiomen Indians would be their first opponent in District play. The winner would go on to face the favorited Strath Haven in the final. The loser would go home.

With just seconds left on the clock, Upper Perkiomen was the clear winner in this contest and would be advancing on to the District Championship. The score was 29-19, and the Indians had possession. On what looked to be the final play of the game, one of the UP players raced toward the end zone. His touchdown would put the Indians up by another 6 to 8 points in a demoralizing finish for the Rare Breed.

It was a touchdown that never happened. The naturally talented and competitive LC QB, Big Jim and Mick's grandson, our nephew, Mike deMarteleire, Jr., played both sides of the ball. In a remarkable defensive play, he chased down the Indian player steaming toward the goalposts. As he tackled him, he wound up his arm, and, swinging it full circle, punched the pigskin right out of the Upper Perk's would-be scorer's hands. The Rare Breed recovered the fumble with enough time to deliver one play.

Picture every epic movie where the imminent losers vow to go down fighting. The Rare Breed went to that playbook. Big Jim gathered the team to discuss what would be their final play of the season. One player suggested a Hail Mary pass. It was agreed the opposition would be expecting that call. Instead, the Rare Breed would take the field with one goal in mind: keep the ball alive.

Keep the ball alive they did. In an unbelievable series of seven lateral passes, with Michael getting the ball twice, the Crusaders scored on a Tim Herman touchdown, ending the game in a 26 to 29 loss to the Indians — but one they wouldn't forget.

The following week, the incredible play was all over national television, from the morning shows to sportscasts. And, a few months later, that novel cable TV sports network that piqued Dad's interest some fifteen years before? Well, they give out this thing called the ESPY Award every year. In 1998, ESPN presented the Rare Breed the ESPY statue for the Most Outrageous Play — what they dubbed the "Cal-Stanford play." But it was more than outrageous. It was a play that beautifully captured the spirit of high school football and playing your heart out to the end. That is, sometimes if you shoot for something and if you don't give up…well, you may not get what you wanted, but you never know where you are going to land.

That play became another great memory we had been collecting for years on our ride with Big Jim, Mick, and our ever-growing Football Family. In the beginning, from his very first meeting with a group of teenage boys in the high school cafeteria of a new town, Dad had issued a challenge, and the Rare Breed responded. On our journey, we witnessed heartbreaks, comebacks, triumphs, and sometimes even miracles.

As we were traveling toward the new millennium, we saw our share of triumphs. The Rare Breed had successfully completed a three-peat, taking the league title once again in 1998. Danny, in 1999, coached his purple and gold Cahillites to a Philadelphia Catholic League Championship. It seemed Dan was at the dawn of his head coaching career, while we had to consider that Dad, after 30 years, was nearing the end of what had been his entire life, what had been all our lives, and the only way of life we ever knew. While the rumblings of retirement began in small circles in both our family and elsewhere, there was one person who didn't even allow the word to cross his mind — Dad. At least not for very long.

Every time he saw a new crop of young men ready to take the three fields and play for the Rare Breed tradition, he was energized like the young man who had taken the reigns of the "Faith, Family, Football" legacy a generation before. To him, there were still plenty of places to go — be they heartbreaks, comebacks, or triumphs — for this Football Family.

~ FAITH ~

CHAPTER SEVEN

The Challenge

"For nothing will be impossible with God."

~ Luke 1:37

With the birth of Rebecca Ann Algeo on June 2, 2000, to Daniel John and Courtney Fitzsimmons Algeo, a new decade had arrived. Big Jim and Mick's clan of nine had grown to 14 grandchildren. Sweet Becca was a welcome summer joy in a time when the world survived Y2K and months of American election drama.

As the door swung open to a whole new millennium, George W. Bush became the forty-third American president, after Al Gore conceded over a month after the election on December 13, 2000. I remember that the topic made for lively conversation at our growing Thanksgiving table that year before we returned to the wonderful world of football, both watching the games on TV and exchanging commentary about local high school sports.

Like any other decade, our family marched on with time. Gas was now $1.26 a gallon, eggs cost 89 cents a dozen, and a loaf of bread could now be purchased for an average of $1.72. Then nineteen-year-old Tiger Woods burst onto the sports scene as the youngest player to ever win a Grand Slam in golf, and a young swimmer named Michael Phelps, at only 15, made his Olympic debut in Sydney, Australia. On the silver screen, *Scary Movie* spoofed the rash of nineties' horror flicks, Tom Hanks was *Castaway* on an island for four years, and *Gladiator* took home the Academy Award for Best Picture. Lee Ann Womack sang "I Hope You Dance", Nelly sang some "Country Grammar", and NSYNC sang "Bye Bye Bye."

Saying goodbye to the twentieth century behind us meant facing a whole new world where technology was advancing at an amazing clip like never before seen in the history of humankind. Just years before, the only two phones in our house were the one beside my parents' bed and the one placed in a "quiet" corner of the dining room. Now, phones were small, with flip lids, could be carried in the pocket, and used to send messages with a new thing called "texting".

With all that continued to go on and change around us, our family remained rooted in faith and simple things like a new niece's Baptism, a nephew's First Communion, a grandchild's graduation, an aunt's birthday party, and Dad's football schedule. I moved my son, now in first grade at Saint Stanislaus School, back home to Lansdale to live that kind of life. As technology began to increasingly expand our world to the farthest parts of the globe, there was something beautiful in living a grounded life of mostly joy in an unassuming corner of the earth whose hallmark was "Faith, Family, Football." No matter what chaos might exist in the world, the Rare Breed of Lansdale and its three green fields, our annual summer excursions to Sea Isle, and our gatherings at Saint Stanislaus Church to celebrate life's moments were still the biggest things that mattered. These places remained sacred.

It was around then that one had to begin to wonder if Dad's dream career as a high school football coach was winding down. For a spell, he seemed more tired than usual following a long day in the classroom and on the practice field. A visit to the doctor revealed his heart needed a stent.

The procedure rejuvenated Dad, putting much of the retirement talk to rest. Big Jim seemed determined to live his boyhood dream from the pages of *Catholic Boy* magazine for as long as God would let him. He and

Mom went on maneuvering their way through this new millennium in the same way that they had always done. The week started with an early Mass, after which Mom would prepare a spread of bagels, muffins, and fruit for the men who were about to file in the door to our living room for the coaches' meeting every Sunday of the fall.

The bar that the young and handsome Bernie Shaeffer had set in the late sixties was reached decade in and decade out by a long line of incredible men. Anthony Sandone. James McColgan. Dave Ferenchick. Doug Grunklee. Doug Danenhower. Earl Alcott. Dave Leach. Dan Shallow. Paul LePre. Ray Lagomarsino. Joe Willis. Mike deMarteleire. Mike deMarteleire, Jr. Jim Algeo, Jr. Dan Algeo. John Algeo. Rare Breed Alums, such as John Wagner, Joe Ritinski, John Walsh, Mike Wagner, Steve Adams, Mike Basilii, and John Woehlcke.

Woehlcke, in fact, spent the entire decade of the nineties as Rare Breed, first as a player on the 1990 freshmen team, then as an assistant right up until the year 2001. His own story tells of a family in search of a "Faith, Family, Football" mindset that — again by a newspaper — discovered Lansdale Catholic's brand of football by chance.

"We couldn't afford LaSalle or Prep. At this time, when I was in seventh grade looking for a high school, my mom got to know Al Pauzano through travel soccer with my brother George and his son Mike. He always spoke highly of LC. At the same time, my grandfather was impressed with an article he found in the *Catholic Standard and Times* about LC's football coach with a large athletic family. He loved that the coach named all the girls Mary with unique middle names. My Pop-Pop was my first hero. Coach Algeo became my second as the two men are nearly identical in their character and devotion to their faith. So we went to Noell Maerz's last game on Thanksgiving Day, that 25-0 victory. I was so impressed with this little school that took it to the big local high school. I told my parents I was on board and that's where I wanted to go to high school. It was the fall of 1988, my 7th grade year, and the diocese didn't have open enrollment yet.

"So my parents put their house up for sale in a terrible real estate market," added John. "It took nearly two years to sell but during the beginning of my sophomore year the house sold. In order to register at LC, though, my parents had to provide proof that my house was on the MLS system and available for sale. I look back now, and it was the greatest gift my parents ever gave me. It was the whole package. In one school I saw 'Faith, Family, and Football' before I even knew that to be the program's mantra."

Like John, each dedicated coach had found his way into our living room somehow, engaged in meetings that were well-designed — and often worthy of some eavesdropping on my part. Mickey would go to a mid-morning Mass, then hit the grocery store on the way home. I could hear her fixing the coffee, setting up the TV trays, and prepping the spread of bagels, cream cheese, fruit, and pastries as the front door swung open a handful of times as she did so. In they came, one at a time, the indispensable and anything-but-uniform medley of men, greeting my mom with a kiss and taking their place around the living room, where a large television displayed the previous day's game. It was a far cry from the black and white film projected onto the dining room window shade.

The intense scrutiny over game footage, however, had not changed. Over the next few hours, that game would be reviewed, dissected, replayed, and relived by these gentlemen. Their names and faces may have changed over the years, but their immeasurable value did not as each brought his own personality, his own character to the table as they forged ahead in their brainstorming mission to arm their young team with every weapon possible, every chance possible to win that next game.

Like most families, the back-and-forths, the go-rounds, the rows were just as crucial as the laughter, the consensus, the togetherness. These men, who might just as well have been sitting in peace in their own living rooms watching the NFL with their feet up and a beer in hand, were family. In their unstoppable mission to work together for a common goal, they gave their talents, their energy, their enthusiasm, their time, and themselves to the Rare Breed. Their impact was without measure.

As LC Class of 1987 Bob Culp put it:

"One of the things that I really admire and cherish about my time with Rare Breed is all the good men and all the good role models that were part of the football program. These guys, to a person, were great role models. They were good family men. They were good coaches, and they put all the time they could in — hours and hours. They were out there early. They were out there late. They were good people. They would ask us about our grades. They would ask us about our families. They would tell us to support other teams in the school. We would sometimes take a break from practice and go watch the girls' field hockey team. They harnessed the whole idea, 'It's not just us. It's not just me.' There's something bigger that we're a part of."

Sunday coaches' meetings, Friday night games to the backbeat of marching bands, dripping August practices that gave way to chilly October games...things went on as I had always known them to go since I was a child, and the sometimes craziness of the outside world beyond Faith, Family, and Football never seem able to touch us.

That all changed one Tuesday morning in September.

The day started like any other Tuesday of the nearing autumn season, ironically ordinary, with school buses filling the roads after a summer-long hiatus and parents rearranging work schedules as their children went to school, some of them for the first time. Big Jim went to Lansdale Catholic High School to teach accounting classes and coach, Mom went to Gwynedd Mercy University to tend to administrative duties, and I stood before twenty-four fifth grade students ready to teach them the difference between "parallel" and "perpendicular."

I had just written those two words on the board, not long after 9 AM, when the principal asked all teachers to briefly meet her in the third-grade teacher's room down the hall. It was an odd request, but my grade partner and I met in the corridor, looked at each other quizzically, and headed to the last classroom on the floor. All the other teachers were standing around a tall cart on which a television repeatedly displayed the horror of what Americans will forever remember as "9/11."

The day unfolded with images and fears and emotions seared into the hearts and minds of many around the world. It is a day, for those of us who witnessed it, that will vividly live in a place that we can draw from our memories and describe as if just yesterday. For us, as for many, it was a world event that went beyond a horrible headline and merely watching from a distance. The inhumanity reached with a sudden, shocking, and insidious arm right into our communities, our backyards, and our homes, gripping families and friends with grief and sorrow.

Lansdale is over one hundred miles away from New York City, but it was not spared the pain of 9/11. Only part of Noell Maerz, a piece of his ankle, was found in the ruins in the weeks after the attacks of September 11th, and yet, to his loved ones, he left his whole self behind in the form of an astounding legacy. The confident and talented athlete who quarter-backed the Rare Breed's messy Thanksgiving victory over the crosstown rivals almost fifteen years before did not survive the destruction of the World Trade Center. He left behind a wife expecting their first child, a devastated family, and friends who, to this day, come together every December to remember him on one of the three fields of Lansdale Catholic, where The Noell Bowl is an annual event. Wearing green and gold, his family and friends gather to engage in a light-hearted flag football battle to celebrate the love Noell had for sports competition.

Just up the ascending fields from where the game is played in winter and through the doors of the school building where most of the players once strolled from class to class, there hangs the green #11 Crusader jersey in its golden frame. It is the only football uniform hanging from LC's walls, following a decision Big Jim made to reverse a 40-year policy of refusing to retire any one player's shirt...until Noell.

The football team attended the memorial service held by family and friends at Saint Stanislaus Church that October. It was understood that the team had a game that afternoon and would have to leave early. What could have been an awkward moment of disruption was remembered as a touching and respectful one. When it was time to go, Big Jim stood up, nodded to the first row of boys, bowed his head, and walked toward the back of the church. The boys were not trained or instructed to do what followed. They simply modeled exactly what their head coach had done, stepping silently out of the pew, row by row, and bowed their heads in reverence before processing in a line around the back and out the doors of the church without a sound.

For several years after Noell's passing, Dad and his crop of up and coming players for the Rare Breed would get up early on a Saturday morning in the fall and volunteer their time to help with a local event established in Noell's memory, the Patriot Games Triathlon. Noell, who grew up in a Saint Stanislaus Grade School uniform before donning his number eleven Crusader jersey, became well known to teenage boys who had never even met him as the embodiment of everything Rare Breed.

September 11th and the death of Noell and just less than 3,000 innocent souls drastically changed our lives, and we were all holding onto our loved ones a little bit harder and longer whenever we hugged in the days and weeks after. We didn't just watch the atrocity, but, instead, we were every bit part of it, which, ironically, somehow inspired more good than evil. We became so much more intensely aware of our blessings, those we loved, the things we enjoyed, the beauty around us — and so less concerned about the small stuff.

During this time, if there was one thing that gave me peace and took me away from the world's troubles, it was the discovery of the joy of camping and cabining. This penchant for finding hiking trails across the state, unfortunately, pulled me away from many of Dad's games. In the early part of the 2000s, I had missed several Rare Breed contests, as I spent almost all my weekends pitching tents and building fires around Pennsylvania and sometimes New Jersey or even New York.

I knew well from our family drives to games all over the state for over thirty years the beauty of Pennsylvania's landscape. From the Intercounty League games in "God's Country" of Berks County to the quaint and picturesque communities of the Bicentennial League to the rolling rural hills and farmland still preserved in the growing suburbs of the Pioneer Athletic Conference, the loveliness of the Keystone State was already familiar to me. My days in tents and log cabins built as long ago as the Great Depression only expanded my journey to even more gorgeous settings, sometimes found in the lush green of summer, the pristine white of winter, and the golden colors of fall. From the Pinnacle in Reading or Mount Minsi over the Delaware Water Gap or along the Clarion River of Cook Forest, so many gorgeous places were treasures to add to the travel log that Dad and Mom began from the time I was a child.

One Saturday afternoon in October of 2003, I made the decision that I should go to a football game instead of a typical autumn mountain trip. Mom mentioned that is was the last game of Dad's thirty-fifth season, and something inside told me to go. I was beginning to think that he was coming to the end of his career, and, if I missed the last game he ever coached, I would forever regret not being there.

We had all come a long way since Dad's first game, when his hair was dark and Mom had to pluck Jimmy from our backyard in Aston to travel with six kids to a high school football game an hour away. Nearing forty years of coaching and over two thousand boys now part of the Rare Breed, we were still a Football Family in every way.

My brother John and nephew Michael now joined the LC coaching staff, while Jim, Jr. continued as an assistant at Pottsgrove, our formidable PAC-10 opponent, and Danny had just accepted an assistant coaching position at Cardinal O'Hara High School. Dan's new school, the home of the Lions, was named after Catholic Education leader Cardinal John

Francis O'Hara of the Congregation of Holy Cross, with whom Dad had studied as a seminarian. The cardinal served as President of the University of Notre Dame from 1934 to 1939 and as the Archbishop of Philadelphia from 1951 until his death in 1960. At O'Hara, Dan was taken under the wing of Head Coach George Stratts, who held the distinction of winning two Philadelphia Catholic League Titles at two different schools, Cardinal Dougherty in 1982 and Cardinal O'Hara in 2000.

Danny's first season there was a winning 7 and 3, and Jimmy and Pottsgrove were on their way to their fifth league title. Things were not faring so well for Big Jim, however, this season. At least, that is what I was hearing. Either way, I was going to the last game on the schedule.

The game was against Methacton, who would later join the PAC league and be head coached by Paul Lepre, one of my father's strongest assistants. For the time being, he was on our sideline at one of the last games played at the old, cherished Souderton Stadium.

I had been to one other game all season, which they lost. I really hadn't been paying attention to their season very closely because, when they won this game, there was an exuberant reaction among the LC crowd that felt something like a Super Bowl win. I turned to Veronica, the only Algeo daughter Dad saw fit to put on his staff because she could literally speak about any sport, seeking for her to explain the extreme reaction of the crowd.

"Why are the cheers so loud? Did we win something other than this game? There's no way we're going to playoffs, are we?"

She explained that this young team had started this season 0 and 5, but this win had just given them their sixth consecutive victory and a winning season after what could have been a demoralizing beginning. In true Rare Breed form, established from the earliest teams of the late 60s and early 70s, who played through their losses while firmly planting a competitive and championship tradition that began with the undefeated 1972 season and grew into regular league and district crowns and an improbable

ESPY along the way, the young men pushed through their disappointment grounded in a single-minded approach with words that were literally whispered from the blades of grass on their modest practice fields for decades: "Get. Better. Every. Day."

They did.

The holidays passed and before long, it was the winter of 2004. The offseason workouts and clanging of weights were now in full swing. As a woman approaching forty, I had witnessed the football program's preparation cycle through the changing seasons every year since as far back as I can remember. At this stage, the number of teenage boys who had taken part in the yearly Rare Breed workout regimen was over two thousand since the day Big Jim opened a humble and hodgepodged weight room for business at Lansdale Catholic.

That same winter, in late January of 2004, we were stunned by the news that Matt Walsh, Rare Breed 1977, at the age of 44, suddenly died of a heart attack while playing pickup basketball with his friends. I was told Matt had just leaped in the air to grab a rebound, and, as he landed on his feet, he fell to the floor and was never revived. Matt's passing was heartbreaking. He had left such a strong and lasting legacy at Lansdale Catholic, being literally everything you could ask a young man to be: handsome, intelligent, athletic, strong, gentle, and truly kind and respectful.

His family and friends came together to say goodbye on the second of February on Monday afternoon at the church in the parish next to ours. My parents were somber that day, still in shock that such a vibrant young man would suddenly be taken from his loved ones. They loved Mr. and Mrs. Walsh dearly, and they were devastated to watch them bury one of their sons.

It was a hard day, and, right after the Mass, Dad and Mom had to go to his own regular medical check-up. While there that afternoon, Big Jim recalled that the visit to the doctor was basically standard until the very last minute. As he was getting off the table, his doctor asked him if there was anything he was experiencing that he wanted to share with him or ask about. Dad told us that normally, it was not like him to say anything. But that day, he was moved to add one more thing before leaving the office.

He informed the doctor that he had been having a funny taste in his mouth, like...like metal. Upon hearing that, the doctor sent him immediately over to the hospital for testing. Mom began calling all of us to calmly tell us of the situation. I still have the worn index card that I wrote on as she spoke. I wrote each bit of detail, as I sat at my desk at school, drawing in steady breaths and taking notes until I understood what she was saying.

Lots of blockage...open heart...three main arteries...bypass...risk factors low...no other conditions...call Uncle Dan and spread word...

Everything happened so fast. Before we knew it, Big Jim was preparing to have his chest broken open to remove the five blockages in his heart he did not know he had until just hours after Matthew Walsh's funeral. Had he not said anything at the last second of his visit, he would have left the doctor's office with an unknown death warrant.

I will always know someone was looking over him that day, and I will always know who it was. Thank you, Matthew Joseph Walsh.

Things moved so quickly from the moment Dad revealed his unusual symptom. Everyone was there at the surgery that morning, with the exception of Veronica and me. Saint Jude School was just miles away from Doylestown Hospital, and, if anything should happen, we were just moments away. I remember that, as we both arrived at school that morning, a swarm of our very kind and concerned colleagues came toward us down the hall. I left Veronica to meet them to describe what lie ahead that morning, as I took a back stairwell to avoid any encounter that would cause me to lose composure. From the first seconds that I had written down Mom's words on an index card, I was set on believing everything was going to be okay. Until it wasn't.

But on a cold February day in 2004, everything *was* okay. The doctors were pleased with Big Jim's operation, and I couldn't wait to pick up my son and get to the hospital. Our school nurse, Randy, made sure we knew just what post-surgery looked like. Not pretty. He would be ghostly white with tubes coming out of him, she told us, but we should know that is normal.

Knowing this, I gave my son, now ten, the option of not going in the recovery room to see Dad. He wanted to, he assured me. Still in his uniform and fresh from the Saint Stanislaus School car line, he was sure he wanted to see Pop-pop. When we entered, we saw Big Jim just as Nurse Randy described he would be. It didn't faze me, I was so happy he was alive. My son, on the other hand, got upset. He was convinced his Pop-pop was dying.

Suddenly, hearing my son cry, Big Jim raised his finger in the air and declared confidently:

"Don't worry, Dillon! I'll be back!"

Our whole family was overjoyed that the blockages had been detected in time, and the surgery was a success. A steady stream of visitors came to share in the good news over the next several days and weeks. From opposing coaches to the parish priest to colleagues and players, we felt the power of the extended family that expanded way past the 526 living room.

It was the living room that Dad made his headquarters for the next few months. He stunned all of us when, after so many years refusing to miss a day of teaching, he decided to take the rest of the year off to recover. It seemed that maybe he was warming up to the idea of finally retiring.

Big Jim spent a lot of time resting in his armchair that spring, watching the Phillies fervently and following all of his doctor's orders, which included plenty of fresh bowls of fruit and daily walking. He was not allowed to take the walks outside and he didn't have a treadmill, so, instead, he turned our house into a sort of indoor track where he marched religiously from the front door to the back, passing through our living room, dining room, kitchen, and back porch before turning around to reverse his course.

Watching his persistent dedication day after day, it was clear to all that retirement was the furthest thing from his mind. He had been issued a challenge, and, just as he had demanded of over two thousand boys in his charge, he was responding as they had. He was far from the brand-new young head coach just starting a family, but was now the white-haired veteran of thirty-six seasons and twenty grandkids who had just survived a brush with death.

In the months that followed his ordeal, I noticed he seemed to talk about death from time to time. Once, he told me a story about one of his afternoon football practices. As he was coaching his players, he had his back to a long line of trees at the end of the field. They were facing the trees, beyond which was another large field. He noticed the eyes of the players being diverted away from his instruction, following something in the sky behind him. Their jaws dropped and so did all attention to Big Jim, until Dad turned to see what they were looking at: a small airplane falling from the sky and headed straight to the open field behind them. It crashed.

The whole team raced to the scene of the accident, certain it would be a tragedy. But, when they got there, two men were almost casually emerging from the plane with nothing but a few scratches. They survived. It wasn't their time.

Dad understood that it wasn't his time either. If he was still here, he was here for a reason. God wasn't finished with him yet. Every passing month, as he walked from front door to back, there was a light in his eye and a skip in his step that was beginning to reveal an undeniable fire in his belly. There was a voice inside him driving him on. It is not a movie he would likely ever watch, but, as I watched him moving back and forth through the house, I could literally hear Rob Schneider's *The Water Boy* Townie encouraging Dad with every step.

He marched and marched that household route day after day, until one day he marched into school to announce he would be returning to the classroom and his three green fields for another football season.

When our vacation at the shore ended in 2004, it was business as usual for the Football Family. Having ending the previous year with six straight wins, the coaching staff and team came back to August camp with four words stretched across the back of this year's practice shirts: "Finish What We Started."

The Catholic Boy was not done yet.

CHAPTER EIGHT

The Comeback

'For I know the plans that I have for you,'
declares the LORD, 'plans for welfare and not
for calamity to give you a future and a hope.'

~ Jeremiah 29:11

When Mary Margaret Filliben married James Michael Algeo on October 17, 1959, she knew what he wanted to be. When he proposed, he told her he was sure of three things. He wanted to teach and coach high school football. He wasn't going to make a lot of money. He wanted her to be by his side as his wife.

Before that moment, Mickey had pondered the idea of studying nursing, but, as high school graduation approached, she decided she would be fulfilled as a wife and mother. Eventually, she became wife to Big Jim and mother to nine children. To this day, I am not sure any course of study would have prepared her for all that her job entailed.

In almost sixty years of marriage, Mom would learn how to drive a school bus, become a secretary, and earn an Associate's Degree. Perhaps the most admirable skills she would learn, however, were the ones that were largely self-taught. She would get under cars, dismantle the back of a broken washer, knock down walls, and attempt to fix anything that was broken, from the plumbing to the lawn mower, on her own before ever summoning or paying for someone else to do it. She was very often successful.

Mickey learned to be quite handy, and, in addition to her prowess for fixing things, one of her learned skills was the ability to build things. One task she undertook was the building of two long shelves that she put up in her and Dad's room. Over the years, these shelves collected and held very special keepsakes, some from football, some from family, and, of course, some from faith.

One item I distinctly recall sitting on one of those shelves was a big giant book set. The slipcase that held two big books inside was large, standing at least a foot high. On the outside was a picture of a man in a beige coat, a dark hat, and a pair of glasses. Under his arm, some kind of paperwork was tucked, and, on his face, was a big smile. In that smile was a gap between his two front teeth.

When I pulled the books out of the case, one read *Vince Lombardi on Football, Volume I,* and the other read *Vince Lombardi on Football, Volume II.*

The first I ever heard of Vince Lombardi was as a five- year-old when Danny rather confidently declared to me that, "Winning isn't everything. It's the *only* thing." When I asked him who told him that, he answered me as if I should already know this.

"Vince Lombardi!"

My second encounter with Vince Lombardi was in our family living room when I was six. I was getting ready to join the family to watch whatever our regular selection of television shows was for that evening. I can't say for sure what they were supposed to be that night, but I remember that, to my dismay, Dad suddenly seemed interested in turning the channel to something else.

Back then, there was no cable TV or streaming, no video players or DVDs, and no way to watch a movie or show unless you went to a movie theater or saw it on the television. You had three networks, three local channels, and one public broadcasting option. That night, a made-for-TV film aired that, oddly, I would never see aired again. To this day, it is not shown on cable, isn't available on DVD, and, when one wants to view it on demand, must watch a grainy YouTube version that is missing a quarter of the movie.

Like many other things I didn't go for at first, I didn't like watching something other than our regularly scheduled program for that night. In the end, however, I am glad we had the chance to watch *Legend in Granite*, which starred Ernest Borgnine as the legendary Vince Lombardi.

The scene that made the strongest impression on my six-year-old mind was when Lombardi fined Max McGee, whose character narrates the story, five hundred dollars for breaking team curfew. (Dad also had a strict curfew, and no one in my family will *ever* forget when one of his players broke it because he was on a date with our sister.) It struck me that he was coming down very hard on McGee and maybe even being a little overly mean at the time. In hindsight, he was pushing his players to exceed even their own expectations and achieve excellence.

"I firmly believe that any man's finest hour, the greatest fulfillment of all that he holds dear, is that moment when he has worked his heart out in a good cause and lies exhausted on the field of battle, victorious," was one of Lombardi's many profound quotes.

As time went on, it was clear to me that this mindset had become the rock embedded in the foundation of the Rare Breed football program. The ride to excellence often requires a lot of pushing and pulling, sometimes yelling and sometimes soft-spoken tones, but always leading, relentless hard work, and complete and utter heart. I had never witnessed anything less.

In the case of Vince Lombardi, like my Dad, it all depended on the presence of his family. Early in the film, when Vince believes he will never achieve his dream of being a head coach with the New York Giants, where he was an assistant, he begins to seek the position elsewhere. He lands in

Green Bay, Wisconsin, one thousand miles away from New York City. His wife is not crazy about moving their family to such a drastically different city.

In a very tender scene, Vince, who at 45 believes himself to be a failure, tells Marie he needs his family there. If his family is not going to be part of it, then he is not going to Green Bay. Marie lets him speak his peace before finally telling him that there is no possibility her husband is going anywhere without them. I understood her response well. This is the life of a football family.

We had already been to so many places, and we were all prepared to go many more now that Dad was given a clean bill of health and another shot at life. In fact, in the months after his surgery, we had journeyed out to Hershey as a family to watch him be inducted into the Pennsylvania Scholastic Football Coaches Hall of Fame in July of 2004. Now, we were set to go with him as he embarked on his thirty-sixth season at Lansdale Catholic.

The return to football came on an early Friday in September. Mom, Dillon, and I arrived early. I vividly remember the first game of that season was a beautiful evening, and I can recall its sights, sounds and smells typical of a Friday night high school football game. The players warmed up, the refs were stretching, the band was tuning its instruments. The late summer day was turning into night as the sun was setting, lighting the sky into a quiet fire of pink and orange hues.

It didn't take the Rare Breed long to get on the board, as they scored a touchdown I won't forget, with a young man named R.C. Lagomarsino crossing the goal line into the end zone, his index finger pointing in the air, the universal declaration for, "We are number one." I smiled at the gesture, thinking how it was maybe somewhat premature to be announcing first place status. The season's first points were posted on the scoreboard, and LC went on to win their first contest, 40 to 0.

It would not be their last win, nor would it be the last time Raymond Clayton Lagomarsino crossed the goal line to score six points for the green and gold. If the 1980s brought Marty Roddy and his unusual size to the Rare Breed program, the new millennium brought the 5'10" and 165- pounder R.C. and his brand of elusive speed not yet seen to the three fields of Lansdale. Along with him, he brought a father, Ray, Sr., an assistant coach, and his gifted younger brother, Drew.

While the Lagomarsino's were new to the program, the ties from the 2004 roster to LC history were strong, including Nate Kraynak, Bob Ryan, Michael Adams, Eric Quinn, Brendan Fitzsimmons, and Sal Nocchi, whose uncles, the DeFinis brothers, were among the first ever Rare Breed. His mom, Marguerite, was an LC graduate and classmate of Maggie's who led the cheerleading squad. Bob and Greg Walsh were nephews of one of my best friends from my Saint Stanislaus days.

Connections were heavy to the past, but so were LC's fresh crop of new names. Brian Cottone, Matt Moneta, Brendan Bart, and Josh Homa were part of the LC lineup that was loaded on both sides of the ball. That season, another freshman became one of the select few to wear a varsity uniform in the form of the fast and athletic Jimmy Kelly.

I can't remember a season when I watched the Rare Breed barrel through the league like this one. A year ago, the seniors were part of a rough 0 and 5 start. Now, they were putting up scores like 49-6, 48-7, and 48-0 over their PAC-10 opponents. The closest any team came to the green and gold freight train steaming through conference play were the Phoenixville Phantoms, who managed to keep the Crusaders to a 20-7 encounter. The intense battle didn't end without Coach John receiving a penalty for an emotional challenge to one of the official's calls, resulting in my brother running self-imposed gassers come Monday's practice along with any player who had earned a penalty during the game. After a close contest against Phoenixville, the first team to present any kind of adversity to them, the Rare Breed maintained its perfect record of 8 wins and 0 losses, as well as its first place position in the league.

But the team's play against the Phantoms that night lacked the attention to fundamentals that should have been clockwork at this stage of the season. So incensed was the coaching staff at the absence of Rare Breed heart and effort on the field, Big Jim couldn't even muster up a "Good One!" for his team once on the bus. I had never witnessed him foregoing the tradition in almost forty years. After a string of decisive thrashings of their first seven opponents, perhaps overconfidence was overcoming the teenage boys.

The bus ride home was anything but a joyous celebration of victors. Co-captain Brian Cottone easily recalled the exact words of Coach John in an attempt to bring the team back down to earth: "*That* type of effort is not going to beat Boyertown."

The next and ninth game of the season fell on "Mischief Night", the day before Halloween. I couldn't attend because I was at a "spirit"-themed wedding that Saturday. I had gotten so used to LC winning at that point, I hardly expected any other news when I returned home from the blissful occasion that evening. The long faces and sober quiet told me that the afternoon's game was anything but a triumphant event, and it began to seem like a curse had fallen on the team on the eve of Halloween.

Eventually, the miserable details started to unfold. Boyertown won the game by a score of 28-16 in a clash that, by all accounts, was contentious. It wasn't enough that Lansdale Catholic lost to their opponent, bitterly ending any hopes for an undefeated run. What was now haunting the squad was the ejection of two star and starting players, captains Brian Cottone and Raymond Clayton Lagomarsino. When R.C., now such an offensive weapon that he was inevitably a weekly target, retaliated with frustration and was ejected from the game, a heated Brian responded with a punch to the opposing team's player. Both Brian and R.C. were promptly removed from the game.

The mood at 526 following the debacle was grim. Not only was the loss a blow to the smooth-sailing season and a risk to both the conference crown and a play-off bid, but an ejection in the PAC-10 meant that those two players could not play the next and final league game. For Big Jim, John, and the rest of the Rare Breed coaching staff, this unexpected situation meant depending on young personnel to carry the heavy load shouldered by R.C. and Brian each week. The questions now were who and how.

With the ominous Halloween weekend behind them, the Rare Breed faced a challenge they had not seen coming. There was no avoiding that the die had been cast, and they were to play the formidable Owen J. Roberts Wildcats in six days without their captains and two of the best offensive forces in the area. After hours of intense wrangling, the LC coaches emerged from the Sunday morning skull session held in the Algeo family living room with a plan.

The first move was to put R.C.'s brother Drew in at Brian's defensive position, while Sal Nocchi, who had been starting at linebacker, was moved to his offensive spot as fullback. In R.C.'s place, young Dylan Saldutti suited up for him on both sides of the ball. The game was critical, and it was hard to know how the junior sub would handle the pressure of replacing R.C. A win would mean the Rare Breed were outright PAC-10 Champions. A loss meant a multi-team tie for first place and likely negative impact on playoff rankings. More than anything, a triumph would bolster team spirit, while a defeat had the potential to demoralize a group that had been rolling through a glorious season before the last weekend of October and the blundering episode with the Boyertown Bears.

Again, there was another fall wedding to attend, and, this time, our whole family — minus the coaches — was there. During the ceremony, the team was on the field, and, at the wedding, we all anxiously awaited the details and, more than anything, the outcome of the game. Word came as we were sitting at dinner. In a tight competition, Big Jim coached the team to a win, the squad pulling away late in the game to a 26-13 victory and the PAC-10 Championship. We could feel the elation from miles away. The superior score was the least of the Rare Breed's triumphs achieved that day.

In his first start, junior Ryan Sexton stepped up to replace Jimmy Kelly in the secondary, now that the freshman was part of the team's "speed package" at wide receiver. Drew and Sal handled their roles replacing Brian masterfully, while co-captain Matt Moneta, in a timeout huddle, called his own number as running back, assuring his team that he would get the first down on a key fourth down in the final quarter. Perhaps the player who shone brightest that afternoon was junior Dylan Saldutti, who overcame the high-pressure role of filling in for R.C. with a 150-yard rushing performance.

The underclassmen saved the day, the team won their league crown, R.C. would be named the PAC-10 Offensive Player of the Year, and Brian would earn the PAC-10 Two-Way Player of the Year Award. Most critically, the team had found their heart. With the great news, the coaches joined the wedding feast. It went on for hours with an especially festive spirit that evening, and we ate, drank, danced and celebrated love, life, and the victory most of the family never even saw. Mostly, we toasted the wins by each of the players who had stepped up to save LC's incredible season from a potentially disastrous tailspin that day. We were back on track just in time for that most wonderful time of the year, the Pennsylvania high school football playoffs.

*

The thing about high school football playoffs is that you prepare your heart out to win, but, if you lose, your season comes to a crashing halt with tears pouring everywhere upon the realization that you will never be playing football with that group of boys again. The final whistle blows, and the losing team's seniors face the reality that their high school careers have ended, never again lacing their cleats to play on fields where the unique experience that is high school football happens.

In the state of Pennsylvania, at that time, only four teams were spared the heartbreak of a season-ending loss — the ones that won the state title game in early December. The path to that game is both a hard journey and a rare one, and it begins way before August. There are no guarantees. A perfect record or just a decent one can mean nothing in the postseason, and the only thing that matters is what either team brings to the field on that given game day.

Big Jim didn't like to think or talk beyond the opponent the Rare Breed was facing in the moment. It was never his style to predict his team would win a league, district, or any kind of crown. Often, he would downplay what he thought his team's chances were of winning anything, focusing only on the daily grind on LC's three fields and preparing for the opposition with nothing but absolute respect.

Over two months had passed since R.C.'s first touchdown on a warm September night. It was mid-November now and so much darker and colder, but he and the Lansdale Catholic Crusaders were packing heat in their playoff opener against Northern Lehigh. R.C. had amassed over 2,000 yards on the ground in regular season play, and he was flanked by team-mates that excelled in nearly every position surrounding him.

The only exception was that of kicker. For all the talent the Crusaders brought together on one team, kicking was clearly its weakest position. Our team had speed, strength, skill, and an amazing work ethic coupled with camaraderie and refound heart, and, yet, we had trouble getting someone able to consistently kick the ball through the goalposts. When someone was able to, it wasn't always pretty. Dad had anyone willing to try step in and practice. Captain Nate Kraynak responded to the call, fulfilling his duties as a team leader, a wide receiver, a defensive back, and, now, a kicker.

This slight imperfection didn't impact the Rare Breed as they launched playoffs with a win over the Bulldogs, 33-6. In his first game since his ejection, Brian racked up four touchdowns and ran for 130 yards. Northern had come into the rainy matchup with just one loss all season.

Their single defeat came at the hands of the Saucon Valley Panthers, who had successfully delivered their fans an undefeated 10-0 regular season. Having beaten Pine Grove in their first round of playoffs, they were our next opponent. In round two, we were facing a team who had accomplished the rare feat of eleven straight wins. I knew since I was a kid that this not an easy thing to do.

I had heard of Northern Lehigh before, as we had faced them in the mid-nineties' playoff run. They were nearly sixty miles to our north, but, this year, they had to come to us, as LC was awarded home field advantage. On the other hand, Saucon Valley was only about thirty miles above us and less than an hour away. Still, I had never heard of them until late November 2004, when LC would be traveling to their home territory as the visiting squad. Their perfect record made me nervous, and I wondered if the Rare Breed's encounter with them would be the end of the line for our group of boys.

On a rainy, muddy Saturday night, Saucon Valley, the District 11 Champion, shot out of the starting blocks with an amazing 65-run score by tailback Bill Binczak. With that dynamic start, the Panthers' Binczak broke his school's single-season scoring record. In teeming rain that lasted the duration of the game, they would score only one other touchdown that night.

The Rare Breed would get on the board six times, fueled by R.C.'s four touchdowns in a 261-yard performance. Two extra point kicks were missed, but compensated for by Mike Adams' two-point conversion pass to Matt Moneta. Brian Cottone was also having another strong night, scoring once and recovering a fumble.

Where some seniors' seasons end with the heartbreak of a playoff loss, Brian's came to a finish that night in the rain at the start of the second half when his leg became crushed between a linebacker to his one side and the weight of the rest of the line to his other side. When the linebacker finally released, Brian fell to his back, his teammates Scott Hill and Mike Opdyke trying to pull him to his feet. He limped off the field.

The pain was like a bullet to his leg, though he was optimistic that it was just a bad sprain. The coaches decided to sit him out the rest of the game, the team went on to a 42-14 win, and he went home to ice the injury while watching *The Big Ticket*. Few things had the power to wake him from his sleep, particularly after a game, but the agonizing pain in his lower leg had him up in the middle of the night and in the emergency room by 6 am. The X-rays revealed his fibula was broken in three different places.

Without Brian, the Crusaders lost the league Player of the Year and a first-team All-State linebacker, but they did not lose their leader. He let neither his injury nor his disappointment of not being on the field deter him from fulfilling his role as the co-captain his team voted him to be. He understood that leadership, not pity, was needed as the team advanced another week. In playoffs, moving on meant more challenging competition from teams often mysterious and unheard of from other parts of the state.

The unknown team the Rare Breed was set to face on Black Friday came from almost a hundred and twenty miles north of Lansdale. The Lakeland Chiefs were the District 2 Champions, undefeated, and the size of a college team. Their offensive line combined for a collective 1,200 pounds. At least the Crusaders would have the home field advantage.

The game was scheduled for the day after Thanksgiving, the last Friday of November. For Big Jim and Mick's children and grandchildren, we would not be able to attend the annual family prayer service hosted by my Aunt Bonnie and Uncle Dan. We knew our big clan would be praying for us, but we would miss the spirits and song, and the little ones would miss the storytelling and singing by Santa and Mrs. Clause, who gave out the first Christmas gifts of the season to all the children at the gathering.

The Lansdale Catholic Crusaders delivered a gift of their own that night, refusing to be pushed around by the perfect giants they faced that misty November evening. Sal Nocchi, who had earlier in the season stepped in for Brian Cottone, did so again at fullback, scoring one of five touchdowns for the Rare Breed. In a well-balanced offensive attack, quarterback Mike Adams orchestrated a 33-0 win that saw R.C. score twice, with Brendan Brett and freshman Jimmy Kelly registering touchdowns of their own.

The reality that Dad and the team were heading back to a state semi-final as they had done almost ten years ago with John Patrick's squad was starting to set in. One more win was all it would take to finally make that road trip to the final state title game at Hershey Stadium. We had come so close...would we be able to do it this time? Who were we up against next? What kind of team were they? If they beat us, would Dad, now 68 years old, ever have a chance to get to Hershey again? Most coaches don't get even one chance there, let alone a second.

All these questions would have to be put on hold for another day, as we left the stadium and headed back to 526 to savor and celebrate the win. Besides, Santa had discovered the kids of the family couldn't make it to the traditional prayer service with the rest of Algeo clan, so he had found his way to Lansdale. When we arrived at Big Jim and Mick's after the game, St. Nick had left their presents in the family living room, along with congratulatory notes on the big win. It was time for family and for children to open presents, and football would have to wait until tomorrow.

*

In the year 2004, Big Jim and Mick had been married forty-five years and, nine children later, now had sixteen grandchildren. That same year, former President Ronald Reagan passed away, Olympian Michael Phelps won six gold medals in Greece, *Friends* went off the air, and Usher's *Yeah!* was number one on Billboard. In groundbreaking cinema, Jim Caviezel starred in *The Passion of The Christ*, graphically depicting Jesus Christ's violent journey to the cross. The average price of a movie ticket was now $6.21, up from 51 cents since the year Mom and Dad married. Gas was $2.10 a gallon, the same unit of milk went as high as an average of $3.73, and a dozen eggs averaged a cost of $1.34. On December 4, 2004, Dad's team would face the Littlestown Thunderbolts at Coatesville Memorial Stadium.

Leading up to the state semi-final, the first LC had been to in nine years, more research had to be done on the opposition. Littlestown was another team most of us in Lansdale had never heard of. They were situated to our west, just outside of our state capital of Harrisburg, 150 miles and nearly a 3-hour drive away. With each passing playoff week, John Patrick, the defensive coordinator, seemed to stay up an additional one hour later to study the unfamiliar opponent's game film on the little VCR TV in the family kitchen. One morning, we found him in front of it at 3 AM, determined to help coach the squad through this last barrier to the state final. He had been there once before.

The showdown between the last two teams standing in the East was scheduled for noon. Our family, so excited after everything our parents had been through the past year, decided we would plan a tailgate in the Coatesville parking lot an hour before kickoff. It was one for the ages, with everybody bringing their A-dish to the spread. Chili, fried chicken, tomato pie, hoagies, and all kinds of delicious foods I would have devoured any other time. This time, I was too nervous to eat a thing. Mr. Grunklee, my freshman history teacher and the day's announcer, strolled by our pre-game meal and agreed to eat the share I couldn't bring myself to. With a big pit in my stomach, all I could do was think about the game.

Littlestown traveled almost two hours to Coatesville. They entered the stadium as the District III Champions with an 11-2 record. The two losses had been sustained early in the season, and they were now on a ten-game winning streak, including an 11-quarter shutout run.

We scored first, but before it was over, the Rare Breed fumbled the ball four times and missed three extra points. Unlike the previous playoff games, we only managed two touchdowns by the time the teams reached the fourth quarter. Up 13-0, there wasn't a single LC coach, player, or fan who didn't believe that the Thunderbolts could strike at any second and launch a late-game comeback.

As the final quarter began, Littlestown's Evan Hanchett recovered a Crusader fumble at our 43-yard line. With 10:37 in the game, momentum shifted in the Thunderbolts' favor. There was plenty of time on the clock for the opponent to score not just one, but two touchdowns. If we didn't answer, and they knocked both extra points through the goalpost, our dreams of Hershey would be left on that field — along with our hearts.

From the time I was an infant, I attended hundreds of high school football games, and I remember many incredible plays. The one I will carry with me forever is "The Moneta Moment". With just over 9 minutes left, Matt Moneta intercepted a Thunderbolt pass and ran 56 yards down the field for a touchdown. Before he even reached the end zone, tears were rolling down my face and dripping off my chin. I knew, in that moment, God was sending Dad and the Rare Breed to Hershey for a chance at the state title.

In the remainder of the fourth quarter, each team traded touchdowns, Brock Harner of Littlestown getting his team on the board and Mike Adams of LC finding Brendan Brett for LC's final score. The game ended with a state semi-final win for Lansdale Catholic, 25 to 7, but the contest was much closer than the scoreboard displayed. The obvious was not missed by the Crusader fans, who the Thunderbolts had to pass on their way out of the stadium. They received a standing ovation from the Football Family.

As Hershey kisses were being tossed from the stands onto the LC sideline in celebration, the fans came down to find their loved ones and smother them with hugs. The energy on the field was electric. In the crowd, I met up with Big Jim, whose first words to me were, "Where's your mom?" For a few seconds, we had lost her in the crowd, but then she suddenly emerged, grabbing Dad's face and kissing him.

Now I could eat.

I don't remember what a bag of Hershey kisses or Hershey's assorted miniatures cost on December 4, 2004, and it wouldn't have mattered anyway. On the way to Mom and Dad's house to celebrate, we bought almost forty dollars' worth of Hershey's candy at a drugstore in Lansdale. Since Big Jim always parked in the back of the house, we made a trail of Hershey candy of all kinds from the back door to his chair in the living room, the very same trail he had marched back to health on only months before.

While we waited for his arrival, we turned on the TV to find the Philadelphia Catholic League Championship televised on Comcast. The same day that Dad was competing for a chance at the Pennsylvania State Football Crown, our brother and his Cardinal O'Hara Lions, not yet in the PIAA system, were facing three-time champions, the St. Joseph Prep Hawks. Less than two months before, in regular season play, the Hawks had defeated the Lions, 12-7.

My sisters and I watched the game with pride. Danny had come a long way since the days when we tried to revamp his wardrobe. There he was, looking, as we called him, dapper, in his Marian blue sweater, coaching his team to an upset at Villanova University Stadium, 14-13. As Big Jim was following his trail of Hershey kisses to his favorite chair, Danny was winning the Philadelphia Catholic League Championship. This day was easily one of the greatest days in my football family life.

As we ate chocolate and celebrated on the eastern side of the state, somewhere on the western side of Pennsylvania, a quiet team had just surprised their heavily-favored semi-finalist opponent. I had heard of the Tyrone Golden Eagles only weeks before, as the possibility of our reaching Hershey Stadium for a shot at the title started to take shape. The state message boards were on fire during those weeks, and they were peppered with the name of Tyrone football. But as the Rare Breed was wrestling with Littlestown for the coveted bid to the state final, Tyrone was falling to an unassuming victor, the Eagles of Grove City.

On both sides of the state, the Sunday morning papers blared the news of their triumphant local teams. Grove City, just outside of Pittsburgh, was hailed as the Cinderella team of the West. On the East, *Intelligencer* newspaper photographer Rich Kennedy perfectly captured the joy of Mom holding Dad's face in the aftermath of the semi-final win, as the headlines jubilantly announced in big, bold letters that the Lansdale Catholic football team was heading to Hershey.

To see the local newspapers bursting with stories and photographs of the Rare Breed's triumph was overwhelming. It was astounding to think how far Big Jim and Mick had come together since Dad saw Mom on the steps of my grandparents' house. It was a newspaper that held a little bitty job advertisement that Mom found buried in the Classifieds when hope to fulfill a dream had been but lost. Almost fifty years later, now this. They could not know it would all lead to this adventure with newspapers and radio abuzz with excitement.

On Sunday, after Mass at Saint Stanislaus, the preparation for the final clash between the two best teams in the state was underway. It started with a car ride. Head Coach Jim Algeo of Lansdale Catholic and Head Coach Jeff Bell of Grove City agreed to the essential exchange of game video in a friendly swap at a midway point between the two schools. My brother-in-law, Coach Mike, and Dad drove to a halfway point along Pennsylvania Interstate 80, where they met Coach Bell for coffee at a diner. When they parted ways, they knew next time — and maybe the only time — the men would see each other again would be on opposite sides of the field at Hershey Stadium.

It was a long, thrilling, and stressful week. Grove City, because they had rocked the Western playoff system seemingly out of nowhere, was hard to get a handle on. The coaching staff dissected the game film they had been given in order to produce LC's best possible effort against a team that was somewhat of an enigma. Would the Rare Breed "finish what they started" or would they be also-rans at the ball that was to belong to this Cinderella team?

I had many conversations with God that week. Here was a man, my father, who had dedicated his life to fortifying the faith that young men and their families placed in Him, who was one victory away from achieving a dream most high school coaches will never know. At almost seventy years old, having survived major open heart surgery, and with retirement likely not far off, could God really bring him to the brink of this incredible moment of triumph and let him walk away so close, but empty-handed? I prayed that this would not be the ending of what until now had been a glorious and magical ride through the world of high school football.

While I was praying fervently all throughout the week, the boys were facing their five days of preparation with an all-business attitude. While the enthusiasm of the fans and families and LC community began to gather a collective steam as the big game drew closer, the teenage boys of the Rare Breed tradition were the calmest and most composed of all. With steely nerve, they prepared to have a go at the mysterious Grove City Eagles

Well-wishes, cards, and gifts began streaming into my parents' home on Columbia Avenue in the West Ward of the small borough of Lansdale. Giant Hershey kisses and good luck cards were sent to their door, while voicemails from former coaches, players, students, and fellow teachers were left on their answering machine. A message board was launched by President Jim Casey at Lansdale Catholic that week, and supporters from St. Stanislaus parishioners to LC parents to Rare Breed alum sent their best to the coach and business teacher who had been part of their lives there for nearly forty years:

"Good things do happen to good people...you not only develop good football players, you develop good people."

"The run you are on this year is unbelievable. People are talking about it everywhere I go. Makes me proud to be an LC alum, football alum, and LC parent."

"Best wishes in Chocolate Town! Savor the moment!"

"Congratulations to Coach Algeo and the LC football team. No one is more deserving of winning a championship, Coach, than you and your family. LC football games are one of my most fond memories of high school, and your quest to Hershey has rekindled such happy thoughts. Thanks and good luck!"

"A tribute to a great program and a man who has changed many lives, including mine. Go get 'em, Rare Breed."

"Coach Algeo, it's been a long time since my days at LC, but the great memories of the years I was there and the great friendships and experiences will always be part of me. Even way down here in South Jersey, we heard about your bid for the State Championship. Couldn't be happier for you and the team. All the years you have given to the football program, the students, and the school make you an extraordinary man. I never played football at LC, but I still think I've never been prouder to be an LC Alumnus."

"Time after school from September of 1981 until November of 1984 was priceless to me. It was more than just football. I think I speak for a lot of men who played football for you at Lansdale Catholic. You are the best."

"Coach, it is not the winning that brings us joy, but the winning with class, honor, and dignity that you instill in these young men every day. Please know that you are second to my parents in teaching me the life skills I have needed to be a successful man, educator, coach, and father. Know that you take the field Saturday with many more men than the eleven starters you see before you. God bless and good luck."

Friday morning finally came. The Lansdale Catholic student body, plus the teachers and staff planned a big send-off for their team. Later that day, Dad, John, Michael, Mike, Jr, and Coaches Dan Shallow and Ed Quinn were going to load the bus with a roster of forty-two boys and head to Hershey. The local radio station and sports reporters would not be far behind them. Our family would follow later that evening.

On the morning of December 10, Dad came down the stairs in his shirt and tie, white hair combed neatly to the side, and a large duffel bag in his hand. Mom greeted him at the bottom of the steps. This would be the last time they saw each other until after the game the next day.

I had seen my dad cry very few times in my life. Dan's injury, the passing of each of his parents, an Irish ballad on Saint Patrick's Day ... but not much else was able to bring tears to his eyes. At least, not that I had seen. They didn't know that I saw this moment, but that morning, as he got set to leave my mom to go to try to win the Pennsylvania Football State Championship, he started to cry as he said goodbye. He knew that a community and a whole team history were getting behind him at this once-in-a-lifetime moment, and I heard him say the words, "I don't want to let them down. Everyone has been so good to me."

Mom simply said, "You won't, because you've been good to them."

A long time ago, he had cried when he thought he would never be a head football coach. Today, he cried that he would be a head football coach that didn't bring a trophy back to his hometown. They hugged quietly for a few moments. Big Jim then marched out the back door and into the car to drive to the little Catholic high school in Lansdale as he had done about 13,000 times in his life. Only this day was going to be the ride of our football family lives.

Lansdale descended on Hershey that night. Grandparents, aunts, uncles, cousins, moms, dads, friends, an RV full of spirited alum from the seventies, and classmates all arrived in cars and vehicles with painted car windows of green and gold. The next morning, a bus sponsored by the Panicos, a popular tavern run by an LC family (complete with former players), would be bringing more fans from home. Our family members set out after work, and, when we arrived that Friday night, the first thing we couldn't help but notice was the town of Hershey lit up with the lights of Christmas. It was nearing the middle of December, and it occurred to me that I had yet to buy a single Christmas gift.

The second thing to catch my attention was the sight of two buses, one loud in victory and the other silent in loss. The first of four games, two on Friday and two on Saturday, had already been played and decided by the time we had arrived. The sight of the losing bus was sobering, and I prayed again at that moment that the Rare Breed bus would not be the silent one leaving Hershey tomorrow.

Trying to sleep that night was worse than settling to bed on Christmas Eve as a child. The one and only time anyone in our family was in a Hershey hotel to compete for a state championship had been when I was a fourth grader who wasn't allowed to travel to Maggie's state tournament almost thirty years before. Getting here might never happen again, and while trying to savor the excitement of it all, I spent much of that state title eve praying.

Most of us were up with the sun, looking to burn off nervous energy before the showdown at noon. A delightful conversation in the lobby with the grandfather of Dylan Saldutti, the junior who rose to the occasion to help the Rare Breed win their final league contest, helped release some tension as I sipped my morning coffee. The nearly five hours between sunrise in Hershey and kickoff felt endless until the moment finally came for our caravan of cars to begin our trek to the game.

By now, our family had grown to Maggie and Mike with Michael and Jackie; Jim and Mary with Shannon, Sean, Anna, and Sara; Mary Beth and Scott with Maeve and Moira; Dan and Courtney with Rebecca; me with Dillon; Veronica with her own yet to come; Mary Frances and Jon with Mariah and Jonathan; Mary Eileen and Justin with Rio and Ryan; and John and Christine getting close to marriage and starting their own clan. As usual, nearly every one of us made the journey to the middle of Pennsylvania that day. The few who couldn't be there waited back home, eagerly awaiting word from the Pennsylvania High School Football Championship.

It was an afternoon with blueish gray skies and giant puffs of white cottony clouds in the heavens over Hershey Stadium. Pre-game energy was pulsing from the fans on both sides of the field. The stadium seats were filled with banners and signs and colored faces and hair and spirit wear, with students and grandparents and young children donned in white and blue on the Grove City side. On the Lansdale Catholic side were the colors of green and gold we had been surrounded by our whole lives. The stadium erupted into cheers as both teams finally took the field.

Grove City wasted no time with a seven-play drive that ended with a Jim Jaskowak 9-yard touchdown pass to Jack Valley. Andy Hay kicked the extra point. The Eagles led the Crusaders 7-0 at the 9:57 mark.

R.C. answered back about six minutes later with a 78-yard touchdown. A two-point conversion attempt failed, and LC went into the second quarter down by one, 7-6.

The second quarter began with the Eagles sacking Crusader quarterback Mike Adams, causing a fumble and giving Grove City possession of the ball. They made it as far as the 41-yard line before being forced to punt. The punt took a strange path in the air and somehow landed in negative yards. When the Rare Breed took over possession, R.C. immediately burst down the field for his second touchdown. Another two-point conversion failed, and the Rare Breed went into halftime with a 12-7 lead.

We were winning, but it was anything but by a comfortable margin. Our family had seen many times that halftimes can be a funny (or not so funny) thing, and a first-half team could come out looking completely different, for better or worse, in the second half. Right now, we were all feeling the state title hanging in the balance.

As the Rare Breed entered their final half of the season, Mike Adams kept the ball and ran for a 44-yard touchdown run. Again, the two-point conversion attempt failed. The score was now 18 to 7 until R.C. once again jetted down the field on the next possession for a 78-yard run. His brother Drew kicked the extra point. The duo's effort put us at a fairly comfortable 25-7 lead.

But Grove City was not finished yet. The Eagles responded by driving to the one-yard line, where the Rare Breed defense stopped them twelve inches away from the end zone and took over the ball. R.C. then fumbled the ball, giving Grove City a safety and ending the third quarter with a 25 to 9 score. The fourth and last quarter of the season was about to begin.

It began with Eagle Adam Rudolph intercepting an Adams pass and returning it to LC's nine-yard line. Jesse Alfreno took the ball those 9 yards to make it an eight-point game with 11:43 left to play. The scoreboard showed an unsettling 25-17 contest. We were praying that the Rare Breed would, in the last quarter of many of their careers, be able to play their hearts out for the rest of the game.

Five minutes later, junior Sal Nocchi, standing in for the injured Brian Cottone, ran 6 yards into the end zone, followed by another Drew Lagomarsino kick, to widen the gap by fifteen points. Grove City, the Cinderella team of the West, played to the final whistle, but they would never score again that day.

Who did score a fourth touchdown was R. C. Lagomarsino. As he ran across the goal line with just over 3 minutes remaining, he put his hand up straight in the air, pointing his finger up to the sky, just like he did that very first touchdown of the year way back in September. "We're number one." Freshman Jimmy Kelly put the finishing touch on the win by making a beautiful catch in the back of the end zone for a two-point conversion, and the Rare Breed prevailed in a 40-17 championship game triumph.

The game was not to end without drama, however. It seemed at least one official did not like R.C.'s gesture, which had been directed at no one, and decided to penalize him a second time for "excessive celebration." Two penalties of the kind meant he was removed, to the objection of the fans and the WNPV sports commentators, from his the final game of his high school career.

He didn't depart the Pennsylvania Class State Championship without a loud and long bang, however, setting the all-time title game rushing record of any class at 353 yards. As I write this book and tell the Rare Breed story, the record still stands today.

Three minutes after R.C.'s last touchdown, the journey to Hershey ended with the green and gold of the Rare Breed of Lansdale hoisting the big blue and gold state trophy together before a wild crowd. An overjoyed grin and undeniable afterglow remained with Big Jim for a long time after that day. The well-wishers all week had been right. Good things do happen to good people.

The magic of our ride to Hershey continued as we headed back to Lansdale with the crown. Our radio was set to Jim Church, Jeff Nolan, and Joe Ritinski of WNPV Radio as they covered the team's elation traveling east back to our hometown. As the boys and coaches were interviewed, the pride of winning the championship radiated from the airwaves. Suddenly, as the bus exited the highway into town, the sirens could be heard in the background as the team was pulled over.

WNPV sports announcer Jeff Nolan joked that they were getting arrested for "excessive celebration", but the police cars were merely positioning their vehicles to escort the bus back to Lansdale Catholic. On its way, the 5:15 pm Mass was in progress at St. Stanislaus Church, where members of the congregation reportedly turned and smiled as the festive brigade of champions passed by the church. Residents began to emerge from their houses, some of them filming, others touching the bus as it slowly passed by until it reached Lansdale Catholic High School.

Then-freshman standout Jimmy Kelly, who would go on to rack up 45 wins and know a mere 9 losses in his career with the Rare Breed, recalled the dream moment:

"Getting into Lansdale and having the fire trucks escort us was the most memorable part of that day. Getting off the bus to a sea of people in the LC parking lot was an absolutely amazing feeling."

The LC lot above its three green fields was filled with fans of every age, including Lansdale's mayor, as the bus pulled into the entrance.

Forever etched in my memory will be Big Jim standing at the front of the bus, beaming with pride as his staff and players sat behind him as Mickey waited alongside the exuberant crowd. At that moment, I did not see a 68-year-old man with white hair and once fair Irish skin now weathered by years in the hot August sun. No. I saw an 8-year-old boy living in a dream world wilder than his childhood imagination and looking happier than a kid on Christmas morning.

Only one movie comes to my mind when I remember that day. *It's A Wonderful Life.* And it truly was.

That night was a party to go down in the Algeo Book of Family Celebrations. Friends and family gathered at 526 Columbia Avenue to remember this night forever. My best friend, Laura, and godson, Shane, surprised me with a knock on the door and joined the party. Between 526 and Panico's Tavern, there was food, laughter, music, and toasts. It was a party that lasted until well into the next morning, with the last of us turning into bed at 5 am.

Big Jim and Mick went to early Mass that Sunday, where the entire congregation filled Saint Stanislaus Church with rousing applause. When the rest of us managed to get out the door for last-chance Mass, it was admittedly not our freshest appearance at St. Stanislaus Mass ever, but we were greeted with the biggest of grins anyway. There was a victory to be shared with the people we celebrated Mass with every Sunday, some of them since I was a child, that a coach and a team and their families could put God first and still get to Hershey and come home with the crown.

Wonderful things followed that crown. Both Dad and R.C. were named Pennsylvania's AA Coach and Player of the Year. The Philadelphia Eagles made the Rare Breed their special guests one Sunday home game day. A giant banquet was held in the boys' honor. Every single player, down to the last man, received a beautiful green and gold championship ring.

On the night of the banquet, Joe Ritinski addressed the young men and their families. He had played Rare Breed football for four years, coached for three years, covered Lansdale Catholic football on the radio for fifteen years, and was now invited to be the keynote speaker of the evening.

"You now belong to a unique fraternity, namely, State Champions. Few people can make that claim."

He went on to speak about the "life values" Big Jim taught them, including a great work ethic, teamwork, discipline, a commitment to goals, and the ability to overcome adversity. He explained how valuable those lessons would be to them as they get older.

"At some point in adulthood, you will wish you could hear Coach bellow, '*GOOD ONE!!!*' one last time."

That "Good One" and the joy God gave Dad in winning a state title might have been beyond anything he ever hoped for. It didn't feel like it was a win for just that team, but for every team before it that lived and believed in Faith, Family, and Football. If anybody thought this accomplishment was going to bring Big Jim closer to retirement, they were wrong. He was not about to rest on his laurels and hang up his whistle, especially now. Far from it. He was an eight-year-old boy again, as excited about coaching high school football as he ever had been. He was living his dream. And he was going to keep on living it for as long as he could.

Life was wonderful.

CHAPTER NINE

Our Heartbreak

"And He will wipe away every tear from their
eyes; and there will no longer be any death;
there will no longer be any mourning, or crying,
or pain; the first things have passed away."

~ Revelation 21:4

I was in the third grade when I watched *Brian's Song* for the first time. It came on a syndicated channel one Sunday afternoon as a repeat broadcast after we had come home from the latest Mass of the day. At Danny's insistence, I joined a handful of family members settled in the living room to watch the made-for-television classic. Aired a few years earlier, it is the true story of the friendship between NFL star Gale Sayers and his Chicago Bear teammate, Brian Piccolo. The two men became the first interracial roommates in the National Football League.

One of my many favorite things about the movie is the exploration of the completely different personalities each man is from the other. Gale Sayers, the youngest player to be inducted into the NFL Hall of Fame at 34 years old, is portrayed as serious, quiet, and even awkward, while Brian Piccolo is light, outgoing, and, as Gale soon learns, prankish.

In one scene, early in the film, Brian attempts to coach Gale on how to deliver an acceptance speech when Sayers receives the 1965 NFL Rookie of the Year Award. Sayers, upon reaching the podium, fumbles over the first few lines, is unable to complete the speech, and simply thanks the audience for the honor before artlessly exiting the stage. Five years later, however, after his bond with Brian strengthens due to a series of overwhelming challenges endured by both men, Sayers accepts the George Halas Courage Award with drastically contrasting eloquence. His speech about his friend Brian Piccolo is profound and inspirational, simply because he spoke the words from his heart.

I can see why Danny loved the film so much. It celebrates the way experiences with certain people can change a person to become better than what he or she thought they could ever be. Even more so, Piccolo's light-hearted humor, particularly when facing adversity, was a lot like Dan's. One of my favorite scenes is when it is clear that something is very seriously wrong with Brian's health, but no one knows just what it is. Piccolo assures Sayers he knows precisely what is wrong with him. He assures Sayers he is not sick. He tells his friend that he is having a baby.

While James Caan's portrayal of Brian Piccolo does provide some very light and laughable moments throughout the film, the movie itself made me cry in my room for over an hour at the age of nine. Dan felt so bad that he sat with me the whole time trying to cheer me up. He eventually convinced me to come outside and play. I didn't watch that movie for a very long time after that day. To this day, *Brian's Song* is regarded as one of the finest telemovies ever made, and it received many awards and accolades when it debuted in 1971.

Fast forward to 2008. A gallon of gas was $3.39, a US postage stamp cost 42 cents, a gallon of milk was now $3.68, and eggs averaged $1.29 a dozen. History was made as Barack Obama was elected 44th President of these United States. Americans were singing along Flo Rida's "Low" and Leona Lewis' "Bleeding Love", and moviegoers were buying tickets to *Twilight*, *Stepbrothers*, *Iron Man*, and *Forgetting Sarah Marshall*. Also that year, *The Express* depicted the short life of Ernie Davis, the first black player to win football's Heisman Trophy. Winning his own award was Brian Cottone, who earned the 2008 MAC Defensive Player of the Year while playing for Lebanon Valley College, just eight miles from Hershey Stadium, where a late-season injury kept him from competing in the state title game just four years earlier.

In February of that same year, in the Lansdale Catholic gymnasium that had been our childhood playground, hundreds of people were awaiting the arrival of a person who had impacted their lives for the better. Dad thought he was attending a beef and beer organized by the parents of the football team. Instead, he was unknowingly walking into the 40-year anniversary celebration of his coaching the Rare Breed.

Green and gold balloons across tables and tables filled the auditorium from front to back. Seated at those tables were names that had sewn together the pages of Rare Breed history spread over more than four decades. John Wagner, the small quarterback who transferred from Michigan to lead his school to its only undefeated season in 1972. Mike O'Brien, the Werewolf of London, who scored the final touchdown at the whistle to complete the 1978 championship season. John Walsh, his wild teammate, who was part of the well-known Brothers Walsh who left their mark on fifteen seasons of LC football. MJ Grourke, the Lagomarsinos, the DeFinises, the Pinzkas, the Mamzics, the Wagners, the Algeos.

Before the evening full of memories, storytelling, speeches, food, and Irish dance came to an end, one of the first-ever Rare Breed took the stage to speak. Mr. Patrick O'Hara, who had quit football his freshman year, only to come out again as a sophomore, gave the keynote address of the night. Before him were a mix of parents, former players, members of the community, state representatives, opposing coaches, friends, colleagues, and the Rare Breed 2007. The group of boys, led by now senior Jimmy Kelly and classmates Shane Pinzka, Mickey Kahrs, Sean Wojdula, Gus Feleccia, Mike

Selby, and Will Bray, had gone on another state run only months before. Having won the league and district crowns, they advanced to just shy of the state semi-final when they fell to the Dunmore Bucks on a bitterly cold night in Scranton, Pennsylvania, a mere two weeks away from a return to Hershey Stadium. They were now part of a legacy that Patrick O'Hara, Sr., Class of 1970, addressed as he stood before them. In just a few brief minutes, he was able to answer the question of who Jim Algeo was and what he was all about.

"Coach Algeo taught us every day, every game we left the field, to respect and to play the best we could... to practice and practice until we did it right," declared O'Hara before a packed gymnasium. "He gave us a wonderful gift and that was the gift of his good example. We saw it as something that was not just something spoken in words, but lived day in and day out. Take that Rare Breed to college. Take it to your careers, to your families, to your homes. You will be better for it. From his example, draw on that, and hold it, and you will be better for it.

"You can take away all of his titles, but Jim Algeo is the Rare Breed. He made Lansdale Catholic High School a football power. He left his mark all over the school, all over that field down there, all over the state of Pennsylvania. But I think the most important mark he has left on every football player that has played here at Lansdale Catholic is the mark he left on our hearts, and that's the mark of the sign of the cross."

A long, warm applause followed Patrick O'Hara's words, made even more profound by the presence of his own son among the crowd, Patrick O'Hara, Jr. I often referred to the father-son pair as the Rare Breed's "Bookends", as the dad was on the very first of Big Jim's teams, and his son, Pat, was on one of the last. Between the two of them, they embodied just about everything Dad had envisioned Rare Breed to be when he conceived of it decades before.

Young Pat epitomized that natural athletic talent that would find its way to LC's fields through the years, that special kind of player who would see the headlines and get the looks from college coaches. Larry Glueck, Anthony Sandone, Chip Zawoiski, Jim Thompson, Marty Roddy, Steve Roddy, Mike Chermela, Mike Kuhn, Joe Judge, R.C. Lagomarsino, Jimmy Kelly, John Howell. Pat, who would graduate from Lansdale Catholic in 2009, would go on to have a successful career at Division I Monmouth University. He became one of the few Rare Breed players to have ever been offered an opportunity to try out for a professional team, the Philadelphia Eagles.

His father, Patrick, Sr., however, characterized what became the vein of the Rare Breed tradition — the often unknown workhorse who would not play organized football again once he turned in his Crusader uniform after the final game of his senior year. His name would not necessarily be in headlines or on the watch lists of college coaches, but his heart beat fervently in the weight room and played passionately on the field. He was the young man who was told — and who believed — that he could be better than his own limits and expectations.

The names of every player who ever played for the Rare Breed, including my own son — Dillon James Algeo — are listed with their teammates at the back of this book. They all have their own stories. Most of them were not stars or headline athletes. Few of them played beyond their years of high school football. But all of them became the bedrock cementing the foundation of the program, striving to be better every day and accepting the reality that they belonged to something bigger than themselves. Not just football, but faith and family. As many have told me, on those three green fields, they played alongside their "brothers".

Dad would go on to be the head coach of Lansdale Catholic High School four more seasons after that night. In that time, he was named a Maxwell Club Award Winner during an event which we would attend the very next month in Atlantic City, where we dined with Ron Jaworski, Tim Tebow, Dick Vermeil, and Andy Reid. Three years later, we traveled to Grand Rapids, Michigan to see Big Jim inducted into the National Coaches

Hall of Fame in June of 2011. Four months after that journey, a long, story-filled path was about to come to an end.

On October 17, 2011, James Michael Algeo forever retired from head coaching on the fifty-second wedding anniversary to Mary Margaret Filliben Algeo. His mind could coach football forever, but his body was beginning to bend. At 75 years of age, the physical demands of being a head high school football coach were catching up with him. Dad always said that he would know when it was time, and, in a letter to the school principal, former player and assistant coach Tim Quinn, he announced that the last game of the season would be his final day at the helm of Rare Breed football.

The game was scheduled for Saturday, October 29, 2011, against West Catholic High School of Philadelphia, who would travel to our home field, now at Wissahickon High School. Nearly fifty years before, it was West Catholic football that had stopped Jim in the midst of his workday collections, unknowingly drawing him into their late summer practice. The long pause alongside their field that day changed the course of his life.

I woke that morning to run errands all around Lansdale, buying hot dogs and picking up soft pretzels and preparing yet another Algeo celebration to follow the farewell game. Unusual light snow was forecast that late October morning, but, having driven in it earlier, it seemed to me that more snow was falling than anticipated. Mom and I noticed that several other games were being canceled due to the surprise snow, and, as I put my hand on the doorknob to exit their house and head to the game, the phone call came that ours would be postponed, too. It would be rescheduled for Halloween night two days later. There was nothing left for us to do the rest of the day but eat, drink, play, and watch college football. Holding to tradition, the Algeo party would not be canceled.

In a way, it was fitting that Big Jim's coaching career came to an end on Halloween. So many players and students were familiar with his well-known "Halloween" story about the player who went home at lunch to wash his uniform. "Halloween" came back that afternoon with a green jersey instead of a white one, having mixed his laundry with a piece of clothing that ran green dye. Maybe it was a foreshadowing of all the green Dad would see in his future.

Life without that green — and the gold — and the cycle of high school football in his life was not an easy adjustment. Before long, Danny saw that Dad not coaching was difficult for him. As the head coach for Cardinal O'Hara, Dan offered Big Jim a chance to continue coaching young men without the pressure and physical and emotional demands required of the man in the head position. That would belong to Dan. Dad, on the other hand, would become a part of his coaching staff now. It seemed like the perfect solution, and, with their roles reversed, a new path in a new time was being paved. We were still a football family, and the Cardinal O'Hara Lions would become a part of our lives.

By 2014, Dan, with Big Jim as one of his assistants, was approaching his tenth season at Cardinal O'Hara High School. Springfield, Delaware County, not far from where Jim and Mickey had set out fifty-five years before, would now be added to the list of places our travels as a high school football clan would take us. For me, my personal path took me to the Pocono Mountains for those years, as I accepted a position that continued to send me all around the beautiful state of Pennsylvania working with fellow teachers. I traveled as far west as Pittsburgh and sometimes even out of state to New York, New Jersey, and New Mexico. I spent many mornings driving the interstate to Bloomsburg and just as many heading south to Great Valley.

In my life, I can recount so many journeys to so many different places. The one on the morning of July 1, 2014, will be the one I will remember most of all.

As I traveled south toward Great Valley, about to enter the Lehigh Valley Tunnel, which is carved through the Blue Mountains and about a half hour from Lansdale, my mind was thinking of the many things I had to do that day. At first chance, I needed to send a photo I had taken of Dan and Rebecca over a month before when she was the May Queen at her school's May Procession to CVS Photo. Father's Day had just passed, and I had given him a card and a picture frame with a note where the image was usually placed. "Picture coming soon," The picture of the two of them was perfect, and I couldn't wait to get it printed to give it to him.

The Lehigh Valley Tunnel is about 4,380 feet long and takes more than a minute to pass through. In that distance and those moments, a single text came through to my cell phone, which was sitting on the passenger seat. A quick glance over and I saw the word, "hospital." My friend's elderly mother had been in the hospital, so I believed the message to be an update on her. It wasn't. That trip through the tunnel on the first day of July forever changed our lives.

The night before, Danny had a heart attack. He was only two years older than me, just forty-nine years old. He was now in the hospital, in a coma.

As soon as I heard, I went straight off the Lansdale exit to my parents' house. Dad, Mom, Rebecca, and brother-in-law Michael had spent the entire night with Dan, from nearly midnight to seven in the morning, and they had only gotten home a few minutes before I reached 526. No one was on the first floor, so I ascended the stairs. Rebecca was sleeping, and Dad and Mom, who had been up all night, were getting ready to go to Mass. We hugged without saying very much. We were in shock.

The details of the horrible night began to emerge. Danny was taken to the emergency room not feeling right, knowing something was wrong. He had a heart attack while in the ER. For twenty minutes, they could not revive him. When they were able to, they transported him from Lansdale to Abington, where they would slowly try to bring him out of a coma. Only then would we know if he had suffered severe brain damage. It was all so unimaginable.

We all spent that Tuesday, the first day of July, visiting Dan at the hospital. It was so hard to see him that way. Danny, who was so light and humorous and passionate and young at heart...to think he might awaken from his coma and have to live a different life, to recover from such a horrible ordeal. But we started to prepare ourselves for it and began to pray non-stop, as did our friends and family and people in the community. We would be there for him, come what may.

While we waited, we prayed for a miracle.

On Wednesday, I went back to the mountains. Thursday was the day planned to bring Danny slowly from his coma, so Dillon and I would leave that morning. Dil would stay with Jim and Mick, and I would go to work until we could see Danny that afternoon. Veronica and John Patrick stayed with Dan through the night so he would never be alone. We went to bed on Wednesday night praying as hard as we ever had for something in our entire lives.

I set my alarm to go off at five am on Thursday morning. July 3rd. My phone starting ringing before it sounded. The call came in the four o'clock hour. It was Veronica. I was calm as I listened to her words.

"It's over," she said quietly.

Danny would not be coming out of his coma. The doctor would pump his heart long enough for the family to get there to be with him, but she could no longer subject him to the shock attempting to rejuvenate his heart. I hung up the phone after telling my sister not to wait for me, that it was too long a journey from Autumn Mountain to the hospital in Abington. As Dad, Mom, Courtney, Rebecca, and my brothers and sisters arrived, they surrounded Dan and prayed the Rosary.

Danny passed away moments before 5 o'clock in the morning on July 3, 2014.

I did not wake my son right away to tell him the news. Instead, I wailed uncontrollably on my bed alone. I could feel the chunk of my heart that had been ripped out and taken with my brother on his way Home to God, and I sobbed and sobbed until I couldn't cry anymore. The boy who sat beside me as I wept so hard after a movie some thirty years before would never be there to try to make me smile again. Danny, our beautiful dreamer brother with his giant loving heart of light and laughter, was gone.

Just a few hours later, as the boys of Cardinal O'Hara High School football woke up early to attend a summer weight room session, they arrived to discover that Coach Dan was not there as usual. At the door of the weight room, they learned of his death. Shocked and saddened and full of tears, they did what Danny would have instructed them to do. They traveled up the hill to the giant white cross that hovered over their playing field, built only years before. The team gathered around it, joining hands in prayer. As they comforted each other around the cross, they looked up in the sky.

In the blue morning sky of summer, there was a sign for the boys. The clouds had formed a clear white cross above them. Barb Weyler, a friend of Danny's and a football parent, quickly caught the cross on camera. You can see it placed on the front cover of this book under the words *Football Family*. The image and the shocking news of Dan's passing began to spread among all our sacred places and everywhere between to our family everywhere.

*

I traveled from the Poconos to my parents' house on the day Danny died. The inside of the house was empty, but the outside of it was not. Food and flowers filled the chairs and tables of their white porch. It was just the beginning of the outpouring of love and comfort the family that had swelled beyond the walls of our little Lansdale living room would shower on us in our time of grief over the loss of Dan.

At my sister's nearby, my aunts and uncles and cousins came to support us within hours. It never mattered how much time had passed since we had last seen them. We had been coming together in times of good, bad, and ugly since as far back as I could remember, and tonight was no exception. It was just hard to believe that we were gathering because Danny was no longer with us.

I sat with Big Jim and Mick that night back at Columbia Avenue. We all just talked and talked about Dan until early in the morning, laughing and crying, and then laughing and crying some more. He had left us with so many happy moments, so many funny stories, it was easy to laugh. But he had left us. All we could do was cry.

On Friday, our family would join again at Maggie's to plan the funeral. When I woke up that morning, it was all so unbelievable. Our hearts were truly broken as the first full day without our brother had passed. In that time, however, we were surrounded by others, and we were never left to suffer alone. By late morning, there was a knock on my parents' door.

It was Ethan, a young man who had lived across the street with his family since he was six years old. The Bonds had all since moved away, but Ethan, now in his early thirties, came the minute he had heard about Dan. He had come the night before when no one was home, and just sat outside in his car for a long while before leaving. As he sat with us, he talked about his sadness and shock that Danny had passed because "we were...we were all family."

In all the years that the young man had lived across the street, I had never heard him say anything like that. Yet, it was understood. And the family that had grown over the years was not going to let us feel the anguish of losing a loved one all by ourselves. Throughout Ethan's visit, there were several interruptions. Some were phone calls, some were flowers, some were food deliveries.

Another knock came to the door. As my parents talked to Ethan, I stood to answer it. It was Mr. Anthony Sandone, the would-be college player who stayed in Lansdale for his father's business and coached youth and high school football with Dad and Dan. I hugged him and greeted him as he came through the door.

When Dad saw that it was Tony Sandone, he immediately got up and moved toward him. They literally collided in the middle of our living room floor, where they stood together for several minutes without saying a word. These were two of the most masculine men I had ever met, their foreheads almost crushed against one another, and their fists gripping the other's tightly in grief, crying an unspoken pain that did not need words.

When the silence broke, we all sat and continued to just talk, talk, and talk some more about Dan. Somehow bringing out these memories helped ease the reality that he would no longer be physically here with us. As we remembered, there was another knock on the door. It was Danny's godmother and her family with tons and tons of food. They had traveled from over an hour away.

The day ended with us gathered to plan the details of the funeral Mass, to choose the readings and the songs, and to design the prayer card. The prayer card we decided upon was perfect, and I have kept it with me every day since the day they were made. On the front, a picture of Dan, wearing his Blessed Mother blue golf shirt, holding a football, his happy and bright Irish eyes shining and his face showing that gentle smile that we all knew so well. On the back, the Magnificat.

And Mary said: "My soul exalts the Lord,

And my spirit has rejoiced in God my Savior.

For He has had regard for the humble state of His bondslave; For behold, from this time on all generations will count me blessed. For the Mighty One has done great things for me; And holy is His name. And His Mercy is upon generation after generation toward those who fear Him."

The funeral program was also decided. On the cover was the photo I was so excited to give Danny that day.

On the night before the funeral, the prayer cards were given to each person who came to say farewell to our brother. Saint Stanislaus Church, our sacred place where we had celebrated so much, would now be the place where we said goodbye to Danny. We had witnessed so much of our life cycle here as a family...Christenings, Communions, Confirmations, graduations that were all followed by joyous feasts that would last hours into the night. We had shared in those moments with so much of our bigger family — our own relatives, the players, their moms and dads, the St. Stan's parishioners, the Lansdale community. But never did we have to say goodbye to one of our own there until now. And now that family came to share our grief.

They filled the enormous church, the line flowing up and down each long aisle of Saint Stanislaus and out the door into its parking lot and down the street. Many people stood for three hours to see Dan and to be there for Mom and Dad and our family. They were his players, his opponents, coaches, fellow teachers, childhood friends, cousins, college coaches, radio personalities, LC classmates, whole high school teams in their jerseys, the Rare Breed, their parents and siblings, and so many wonderful people who were touched in some way by Danny's life.

Thinking about it made me think of the words Dan Shallow, one of Dad's assistants, had said not long before that day.

"It was family from the beginning."

As the hundreds of that family came to us with hugs and kind words and memories and stories, I would ask those I did not know how they knew Dan. Time and time again, the answer I received was, "We were in his camp at Gwynedd Mercy." This response, which I had gotten from so many that I lost count, struck me as amazing. Gwynedd Mercy was a nearby university where Mickey had been a secretary, we had worked summer jobs, and Danny was a camp counselor close to thirty years before. Not many people I know would attend the funeral of a summer camp counselor they had known a complete generation ago. But, then again, we were talking about Danny. He taught me a long time ago that certain people can change others' lives.

The stream of family touched in some way by one person continued to flow through the church until the funeral director expressed concern that we would be there until well into the morning, possibly beyond 1 a.m. Instead of having them come to the receiving line, he sent us moving through the line of those paying their respects to Dan. Led by Mickey and Big Jim, who marched up and down St. Stan's with his Irish cane, our family followed, thanking the many who came for Danny. Their love lifted us from our grief as if on the wings of angels.

The next day, Wednesday, July 9th, not even a week after the passing of our brother, we joined for his funeral Mass at one of our most sacred and familiar places. The beauty of the Scriptures and the power of the songs truly reflected the life Danny had led and all the things he cherished. And the person he cherished the most gave what became the most graceful and remarkable remembrance I had ever heard.

Dan's childhood friends, Tom Casey and Danny Collins, delivered heartfelt eulogies filled with light-hearted memories and deep appreciation for the loyal, dependable buddy they had lost. Corey Brown, the dynamic Cardinal O'Hara athlete who went on to play for Ohio State and compete in the Super Bowl as a Carolina Panther, spoke of the great influence his former coach and mentor had on his life. He also pledged to Dan's daughter that he was her brother, that we were all family, and she would never have to go through life alone.

It was Rebecca, who had just celebrated her fourteenth birthday only weeks before, who left us with the most profound thoughts about Danny that day. It was hard to imagine that a girl so young who had just lost her father, to whom she was extremely close, only days before could stand in front of hundreds of mourners with such poise and presence. Even as we cried through her words, she remained deliberate and serene, honoring Daniel John Algeo with a remembrance I will never forget.

I will never forget many things about that time and that day. So much of it is vivid to me as we were planning, talking, texting, messaging, remembering, laughing, crying from the single instant that first-day pain seared our hearts.

But there is one moment I will always, always keep in my heart. It is a moment that seemed to stop time. When the casket carrying Danny was closed, we moved with him to the back of the church. There, the whole family lined up behind Dan's close friend, Father John Flanagan, and over a dozen priests who came to celebrate the Mass with him. As we waited for Mass to begin, there was a striking silence. I realized that it was the first moment without a single sound in days.

Suddenly, in one majestic instant, the music and Mass began. The organ was playing, the choir was singing, and the procession began to move toward the altar, with the magnificent crucifix we had marveled at since we were children hovering above it. In a sweeping moment, the robes of the priests were flowing behind them as we marched forward. As the words of "Lift High The Cross" robustly filled the church, a golden cross was lifted high over our procession. Whenever I think of that day, I hear that song, I feel that stirring moment, and I see that cross in the air above us.

Because, in the end, Danny knew something better than most of us. In his short life, he knew that it is always about The Cross — the one above us, the one before us, the one within us. Our faith in that cross would never be more important to us than now.

CHAPTER TEN

Triumph at Sunset

And He was saying to them all, "If anyone
wishes to come after Me, he must deny himself,
and take up his cross daily and follow Me."

~ Luke 9:23

The year 2018 has just ended. The days Big Jim could float on his back in the salty waters of Sea Isle City are long behind him. In fact, he will likely never see the sunrise over the ocean again. These days, however, he can sit on a bayside deck with a cigar, watching the sun slowly descend on another day while the world moves on around him.

Today, the average cost of a gallon of milk is $2.92, a gallon of gas around $3.27, a dozen eggs about $1.76, and a U.S. postage stamp is now 50 cents. The price to attend a movie is just shy of $9.00 a ticket. New York billionaire Donald Trump is President of the United States, the Philadelphia Eagles are wearing beautiful Super Bowl rings for the first time, and the number one song of the year to date is Drake's "God's Plan."

God's plan. I used to be able to keep count of the number of times I have seen my father cry. Since Danny passed, I've lost count.

It's often hard to understand God's plan, but a long time ago, Danny asked me if I thought football was in heaven. I still can't say for sure, and I hope it is, but I do know that there is heaven in football. However difficult we find the plan, God gives us sweet morsels of heaven's joy through little things in life. It could be the euphoria of a hard-fought win, an angelic voice singing at a school play, an amazing sunset over the bay, a compassionate hand in a time of need, or even just a little time cherishing family. And yet, none of it compares or even comes close to His Glory and the days we will spend with Him basking in it.

To this day, our family still finds happiness in sports. Mary Beth and her family enjoy local recreational activities. Mary Eileen coaches youth hoops, while Mary Frances is in her second year as an assistant at North Penn. Now retired, Maggie coached both Lansdale Catholic and North Penn girls basketball teams to a 500-plus victory combination in two decades. Jimmy is an assistant high school football coach. John coaches his son Joseph's lacrosse team. Veronica is preparing her two children for a lifetime full of athletic adventures. The taste of heaven sports gives us is still very much part of our lives.

As for me, I still write, draw, and watch movies.

Big Jim and Mick moved from our childhood home on Columbia Avenue to a smaller apartment only minutes from Saint Stanislaus Church, where both are catechists for the children of the community. Many of the award plaques that hung on their walls and the trophies that sat on their shelves were boxed up, but the crosses that graced our rooms since I was a child remain mounted around them. They now have twenty-one grandchildren to visit them, with Colleen, Joseph, Monica, Brayden, Clare, Scarlett, and Mary joining the clan over the last few years. There are also two great-grandchildren, Brynn and Will, who are the children of Jackie and Bill, who have begun a new generation of family that will take new roads.

Down the street from Mom and Dad is Lansdale Catholic. I sometimes drive by it on the way to visit them. For the past seven years, the LC football team has been coached by Tom Kirk, whose sons were Rare Breed, one of them part of the State Championship team of 2004. With Tom resigning just a few months ago, a new head coach in Dominic D'Addona — who we once faced on the sidelines of former 1980's rival Archbishop Kennedy — has just been hired. Now, a new group of boys and their families will continue to know the bond that high school football brings on the three green fields along a quiet street in Lansdale.

Beside our beautiful St. Stanislaus Church, Daniel John Algeo is buried in a plot my parents had bought for themselves only a few years earlier in a peaceful graveyard. A lovely white fence that surrounds the cemetery separates those who have passed on from this life, including Dan, from children playing games in the schoolyard where we used to run and race and tag each other. In the middle of his tombstone, three simple words are inscribed. "Faith. Family. Football." On one side of it is Mary holding the baby Christ, and on the other side is the Cross. And, today, if you do an internet image search of "the Dan Algeo cross", you will find a picture of a perfect white cross in a beautiful blue sky suspended over the lush green of summer — a reminder that there is life over death.

If only time could be suspended in such a way. But it marches on, and things forever change. And no matter what year it is when you find yourself reading this book, there is just one thing that remains. Always. And that is faith.

A long time ago, fueled by the picture strip he saw in a boys' magazine, Dad was convinced that football could be more than just a game. From then on, he became a student of the sport, mastered it, and learned to teach its skills. Blocking. Tackling. Defending. Receiving. Carrying a football.

I learned there is a certain way to carry a football so that it makes it difficult to dislodge. The player is careful to take the ball with one hand over it and one hand under it. As soon as he can, he pulls the end of the ball back deep into his armpit, where it is tucked tightly as he moves forward down the field. Still, such good form is not foolproof. At some point in life, the ball is coming loose.

In time, young bodies grow old. Speedy young men become slow old men, and the loss of mobility takes muscle and sometimes memory with it. Boys who once moved and manhandled their way around a football field find that one day, though the love of the game may last, the body can no longer play it as it once did. There is no more blocking, running, tackling, receiving. There is no more carrying the football.

I guess that's why Dad yelled so much at the boys with "The Voice", demanding them to play their hearts out while they still could.

When the days of no longer carrying a football come, the days of the family carrying each other remain. No wonder Big Jim and Mick spent so much time nurturing our life together in all kinds of places. Family lasts when football and other things don't. Even then, with time, life takes family, too. As the years pass, we say goodbye. A grandparent. An aunt. An uncle. Our mother. Our father. Our brother. A son.

The only thing that can last, through every loss in life, is faith. When family and football and the stuff of life fade into eternity, nothing can take it away. Dad and Mom taught me that every day. Danny showed me that in his love for The Cross. It is why a magnificent white cross that he helped build stands over the football field where he spent his days coaching the young men of Cardinal O'Hara. It is why those young men turned to that cross when, shocked and saddened, they didn't understand God's plan.

I've thought about The Cross a lot since the day Danny died. It is the place where Christ remained, true to His mission. When presented with every temptation and every chance to unfollow his path, He chose to stay for no other reason than love. It is truly the greatest love story ever told.

Big Jim and Mick are my second favorite love story ever told. In their own small way, in their sacred little corner of the world that stretched from our home in the West Ward of Lansdale to the three fields of Lansdale Catholic to big beautiful Saint Stanislaus Church to the occasional trip along the Jersey Shore and a football game somewhere in Pennsylvania, they lived God's plan.

God has a plan and purpose for everyone. If it isn't a football field, it may be a stage, a teacher's desk, a nurses' station, a courtroom, a kitchen... whatever one's sacred place in the world may be. For Dad and for Dan, it was a football field.

And for a girl who didn't want anything to do with that mission, I sure do miss it now. What the five-year-old kid who didn't want her dad to be a high school football coach wouldn't give for those days to be given back for even one moment. I miss the days that began with mornings of dewy grass and a cool chill that soon gave way to hot and humid practices we watched from a station wagon in the school parking lot. I miss the days that ended with the sound of the local high school marching band drums beating in the distance as the sun began to set earlier and earlier on August summer nights. I miss the days of hurrying home from school on Fridays to eat a rushed meal of hot dogs and baked beans so that we could load into the family car, pray a decade of the Rosary, and sit in stands filled with anticipation and excitement of the unique experience that is only high school football.

As Rare Breed Class of 2008 Jimmy Kelly put it:

"There is nothing that tops the fun we had playing high school football."

There *is* nothing like it, and I will forever miss our Football Family days. The corny jokes we would hear Big Jim tell at the end of practice. The long car rides to distant away games. The "Good Ones" when the team was triumphant. I miss it all.

More than anything in the world, I miss Dan. I would give anything to go back just for a few minutes to watch his passion on the sidelines or to see his unique brand of humor make a whole room erupt into laughter. His funny faces. His singing and serenading. His smile you couldn't resist. The boyish man who could make me laugh in my worst times.

But we can't go back ever. All we can do is cherish the family God gave us and the dreams He put in our hearts. That is our "cross", our mission to carry. It will have challenges. It will need comebacks. It will most definitely have heartaches. But it will end in triumph if we follow that path every day the sun rises. Because the sun also sets.

And when the sun sets on our lives, what's it going to be? Danny Algeo woke up to 18,024 sunrises. But, like the numbers that linger on a scoreboard for a few moments after a game or the statistics that sit in a record book for a time, the numbers don't ever really matter when the sun sets forever. What matters, as Dad and Mom taught, is faith, family, and following the mission God gave you. It will tug at your heart both gently and fiercely until you answer it.

When he gave up his quest to the priesthood in his late teenage years, Dad did not give up the power to passionately preach, by example, faith and family from a football field. In reflecting on the impact Dad and the Rare Breed brotherhood had on his life, Danny's good friend and LC Class of 1991 Kevin McCullagh perfectly summarized:

"The message he was delivering to us was a sermon, *his* sermon, that was not only meant to be executed on the field but to be executed off the field. Ultimately, I think that is what his living legacy is, and is what he meant for us, and now we've taken what he said to the next level. It's been a wonderful journey to try to meet his expectations not only as a football player, but as a young man, and, now, a husband and a father. The field was his pulpit, and his life was his sermon."

For each of us, our own "sermon" is from our own sacred place, wherever that may be. I'm still here. You're still here. Sometimes it is hard to understand why one person survives where another person dies. Yet, we remain here for a reason.

And, as my good friend Mike Stern — who beautifully and warmly opened the door for you to join our ride with his wonderful and welcoming foreword — reminds me, Danny is still here in some way, too. "God Bless Dan Algeo! He will walk together with me, and with every person whose life that he touched, forever and a day!"

The days pass and time marches on. While here, we each get one life filled with some unknown number of sunrises and sunsets. Whatever time brings and wherever the journey leads, make sure, when that sun is about to set on our lives, we can do one thing. Stand up, look back, and be able to say, with all our heart, *"Good One!!!"*

In Gratitude

This book has been a labor of love, and I can never fully express how incredibly grateful I am to many people who have helped and supported me in bringing the story of the Rare Breed Football Family to life through writing.

Thank you, Laura. There is no one I am more indebted to than my best friend who encouraged me to stay the course and make this book a reality so my parents could enjoy it. She and our good friend, Hannah, have been amazing in every way — reading, reviewing, editing, suggesting, but, most of all, supporting. Thank you!

Thank you to my patient son, Dillon, for listening to all my thinking through ideas out loud. So many nights I had to forego watching a movie or just hanging out, and his understanding gave me peace and drive. I look forward to cherishing the time with my favorite young man. It's time we're not getting back.

Thank you to Mike Stern, our lifelong friend and accomplished sportswriter, who graciously wrote a beautiful foreword to the *Football Family* story. I could not have hoped for more.

Thank you to the people who at one point in my life expressed their belief in me to write a book: Ginny, Sister Melanie, Susanne, and Kathy. Your words came at times when most needed.

Thank you to the angels who were there when the journey went off-course for a spell: Shane, Angela, Connie, Chrissy, Tara, Linda, and Kathy.

Thank you to Mr. Jim Casey of Lansdale Catholic High School for his unwavering support and generous donation of time and space toward my research for the *Football Family* project over the years.

Thank you to Jeff Nolan of WNPV Radio and Jeff Fisher of *High School Football America* for constant and consistent support of my project.

Thank you to the photographers and news reporters of our local newspapers, namely *The Reporter, The Intelligencer, The Times Herald,* and *The Pottstown Mercury* for their excellent coverage of high school football over the years, sharing the stories of the joy of sports in both words and pictures. A special thanks to the contributions of Mike Stern and Rick Woelfel, who embody all the best in local sports coverage, and to Al Tielemans, whose sports photography is a true art form.

Thank you to Mark Wolpert and the Maxwell Football Club and all that you do for the game we love.

Thank you to Mr. Dick Shearer and all the volunteers at the Lansdale Historical Society. You were awesome in helping me find every article and every yearbook!

Thank you to Mr. Larry O'Malley for building and maintaining the Friends & Alumni of LC website, which lists every graduate and his or her graduating year.

Thank you to Donald J. Black for the amazing amount of statistics he has maintained for Pennsylvania high school football.

Thank you to all the Rare Breed players, coaches, and family who contributed to the growing archives of quotes and stories through interviews, as well as written memories. Your names are listed in the Acknowledgments.

Thank you to all those who have made a financial contribution to my *Football Family* project. I look forward to resuming sharing the Rare Breed story through the art of film.

Thank you, Steve Adams, for maintaining the Lansdale Catholic Football Alumni Facebook page, a place to share moments and memories and an immeasurable resource for me.

Thank you to my brothers and sisters, so great to grow up alongside and share a wonderful childhood with. I can't thank you enough for answering all my texts when I needed facts, names, numbers, and information to fill in the gaps when my memory failed me!

Thank you, Rare Breed assistant coaches. You served as such great examples of commitment and honor to many young men, and they carry that gift with them forever.

Thank you, Rare Breed, and all the Football Family, for all the wonderful memories, exciting moments, and for living out the *Faith, Family, Football* way of life.

Thank you, Big Jim and Mick for an amazing ride.

And *Thank you*, Father in Heaven, for every good gift.

The Rare Breed

The following team lists have been created using a variety of sources to ensure accuracy. These include Lansdale Catholic yearbooks, game programs, and social media posts requesting review and correction. If you would like to submit a correction, please contact the author using one of the platforms listed on the Rare Breed Connections page.

Rare Breed 1968

Bernie Kunz

Bob Brelsford

Bob Marhalik

Bob McGinnis

Bob Sobel

Charlie Francis

Charlie Peddigree

Chet Wisniewski

Dan Mask

Dave Landis

Don Walsh

Frank Wagenhoffer

Fred Cefali

Gary Shortall

Greg Lohse

Harry Bowie

Jimmy Folkes

Joe Filice

Joe Heppler

Joe Horgan

Joe Peck

Kevin Lohse

Larry Collins

Lou DiCola

Marty Teller

Mike Wynne

Pat O'Hara

Paul Rivest

Rick Wunder

Rocco DiNenna

Ron Meisberger

Steve Collins

Tim Murphy

Tom Breslin

Tom Brown

Tom Filanowicz

Tom Quinn

Tom Rhoads

Managers:

John Monaghan

Mike Grimm

Bill Grimm

Rare Breed 1969

Bernard Kunz

Charles Mamzic

Charles Mastroni

Charles Peddigree

Daniel Mask

David Landis

Dennis Gawronski

Donald Walsh

Eugene Giordani

Frederick Cefali

Gary Shortall

Gregory Lauer

James Flyzik

James Folkes

John Wynne

Joseph Hausler

Joseph Heppler

Joseph Horgan

Joseph Peck

Kevin Lohse

Lawrence Collins

Leonard Kluger

Martin Teller

Patrick O'Hara

Patrick Ryan

Richard Wunder

Robert Sobel

Rocco DiNenna

Stanley Yelito

Stephen Collins

Stephen Parente

Steven Williams

Thomas Ambrose

Thomas Breslin

Thomas Brown

Timothy Murphy

Rare Breed 1970

Barry Isabella

Barry McCarron

Carmen Vare

Charles Mamzic

Charles Mastroni

Charles Veneziale

Chip Zawoiski

Curt Mamzic

David Rhoads

Dennis Gawronski

Edward Kunze

Gary Lohse

Gary Shortall

Gregory Lauer

Harry Gebbie

Howard Cauffman

James Boaman

James Flyzik

James Folkes

James Jacketti

James Nesterak

James Seaton

Joan Jankowski

John Dehner

John Wagner

John Hufnagle

John Wankiewicz

John Webb

John Wynne

Joseph Hausler

Joseph Horgan

Joseph Peck

Joseph Ritinski

Joseph Taylor

Kevin Heppler

Kevin Lohse

Kevin Reilly

Martin Teller

Martin Walsh

Matthew McNally

Michael Folkes

Michael Grimm

Mike Lajeunesse

Joseph Malay

Mike Wisniewski.

Nicholas Thee

Patrick Ryan

Richard Trotter

Richard Wunder

Robert Definis

Robert Sobel

Ronald Langlais

Stanley Yelito

Stephen Pajka

Steven Parente

Steve Williams

Thomas Ambrose

Thomas Brown

John Kozminski

Thomas Darcy

Thomas Grier

Tim Murphy

Vincent Pappas

Walter Albright

William Coyle

Henry O'Hara

Rare Breed 1971

Barry McCarron

Charles Mamzic

Charles Mastroni

Curtis Mamzic

David Rhoads

Donald Walsh

Edward Kelso

Edward Kunze

Eugene Zawoiski

Gary Lohse

Gerrard Kozminski

James Boaman

James Folkes

James Seaton

John Dehner

John Kozminski

John McDermott

John Wagner

Joseph Ambrose

Joseph Malay

Joseph Ritinski

Joseph Stabile

Kevin Heppler

Kevin Reilly

Lawrence Folkes

Lawrence Martin

Lawrence Williams

Matthew McNally

Michael Druan

Michael Folkes

Michael Gildea

Michael Grimm

Michael Wisniewski.

Nicholas Thee

Patrick Ryan

Richard Trotter

Robert Definis

Robert O'Hara

Ronald DiCola

Stanley Yelito

Thomas Darcy

Walter Albright

Rare Breed 1972

Barry McCarron

Craig Rhoads

Curtis Mamzic

Daniel Breslin

Daniel Friel

David Rhoads

Donald Meade

Edward Kelso

Edward Kunze

Eugene Zawoiski

Frederick Wagner

Gary Lohse

Henry Kalinowski

James Boaman

James McColgan

James Seaton

Jeffrey Brelsford

John McDermott

John O'Brien

John Wagner

Jon Blackman

Joseph Isabella

Joseph Malay

Joseph Ritinski

Keith McCarron

Kevin Heppler

Lawrence Folkes

Mark Morgans

Michael Definis

Michael Druan

Michael Folkes

Michael Gildea

Michael Wisniewski

Nicholas Thee

Paul Knight

Richard Trotter

Robert DeFinis

Ronald DiCola

Russell Benvenuto

Stephen Martin

Thomas Darcy

Thomas Gildea

Thomas Greer

Walter Albright

William Walsh

Rare Breed 1973

Bartholomew Lopez

Bruce Stratten,

Christopher Cotellese

Craig Rhoads

Daniel Doorley

Daniel Friel

Daniel McLaughlin

David Lightcap

David Maginnis

Donald Meade

Donald Viall

Edward Kelso

Frances Winton

Frederick Wagner

Gerald Kozminski

Henry Kalinowski

James Kleinman

James Molettiere

James Peart

Jeff Bagley

Jeffrey Brelsford

Jeffrey Morris

John Collins

John Hodnett

John Malay

John O'Brien

John Webb

Joseph Malay

Joseph Monzo

Keith Crawford

Keith McCarron

Kenneth Gustin

Kevin Conwell

Kevin Reilly

Kevin Trotter

Lawrence Folkes

Lawrence Williams

Mark Morgans

Michael Adams

Michael Definis

Michael Druan

Michael Ferren

Michael Guiranna

Paul Collins

Paul Knight

Peter Duch

Richard Carroll

Robert Obermeier

Robert Ryan

Russell Benvenuto

Scott Cooper

Steven Kretchman

Terrance Strobaugh

Thomas Darcy

Thomas Gildea

Thomas Greer

Vincent LaRuffa

Walter Albright

William Kerr

William Kerr

William Ritinski

William Walsh

Rare Breed 1974

Bill Kerr

Bill O'Hara

Bill Ritinski

Bill Steiert

Bill Walsh

Bob Gillies

Bob Ryan

Bruce Stratten

Butch Winton

Charles Glackin

Craig Rhoads

Dan Breslin

Dan Friel

Dan McLaughlin

Don Meade

Don Viall

Eric Groves

Eric Kiester

Eugene Dougherty

Fred Wagner

Gerry McGuire

Greg Famularo

Greg O'Brien

Hank Kalinowski

Jack Hoy

Jaye Fitzgerald

Jeff Brelsford

Jim Blessing

Jim Mullaly

Jim Roos

Joe Monzo

John Busfield

John Carney

Mike Welsh

John Collins

John Higgins

John Hodnett

John O'Brien

Keith Crawford

Tom McGlynn

Keith McCarron

Ken Gustin

Kevin Ferren

Kevin Trotter

Larry Folkes

Mark Morgans

Matt Walsh

Mike Adams

Mike DeFinis

Mike Ferren

Mike Guiranna

Mike Thee

Mike Welsh

Owen Coyle

Pat Curley

Paul Collins

Pete Duch

Rick Carroll

Scott Cooper

Terry Strobaugh

Terry Trotter

Tim O'Malley

Tom Birney

Tom Dwyer

Tom Gildea

Tony Trunk

Vince LaRuffa

Manager:

Martin Thornburg

Rare Breed 1975

Bardo Lopez

Bill Ritinski

Bob Gillies

Bob Obermeier

Bob Ryan

Butch Winton

Charles Glackin

Dan Costello

Dan Doorley

Dan McLaughlin

Don Viall

Earl Alcott

Erich Groves

Eric Kiester

Greg Famularo

Greg O'Brien

Howard Gilpin

Jack Hoy

Jaye Fitzgerald

Jeff Morris

Jim Algeo

Jim Blessing

Jim Kunze

Jim Roos

Jim Wagner

Joe Francis

Joe Monzo

Joe Zobil

John Collins

John Hodnett

Keith Crawford

Ken Gustin

Kevin Trotter

Matt Walsh

Mike Adams

Mike Guitanna

Mike Purcell

Mike Thee

Mike Truppay

Patrick Curley

Paul Collins

Pete Duch

Rich Carroll

Jim Mullaly

Scott Cooper

Terry Strobaugh

Terry Trotter

Tom McGlynn

Bob Francis

Tony Trunk

Vince LaRuffa

Rare Breed 1976

Bart Lopez

Bill Mooney

Bill O'Hara

Bob Gillies

Brian McCarron

Butch Alcott

Charlie Glackin

Chip Allen

Dan Costello

Dan Folkes

Ed Steglik

Eric Kiester

Greg Famularo

Greg O'Brien

Jack Hoy

Jaye Fitzgerald

Jim Algeo

Jim Kunze

Jim Roos

Jim Wagner

John Saldutti

John Walsh

Keith Crawford

Kent Jaggers

Matt Walsh

Michael Murphy

Phil Bochey

Mike Breslin

Mike O'Brien

Mike Trotter

Owen Collins

Pat Curley

Paul Wensel

Pete Duch

Rich Carroll

Terry Trotter

Tim Love

Tim McNally

Tony Trunk

Victor Lelii

Rare Breed 1977

Al Porambo

Bill Shields

Bill Zere

Bob Gillies

Bob Heinsinger

Bob Mayo

Bob McIlhenny

Brian McCarron

Butch Alcott

Charlie Glackin

Charlie Murgia

Chip Serafin

Chris Kretchman

Chris Monte

Dan Kerr

Dave Nentwig

Donny Drakas

Eric Kiester

Greg Famularo

Greg O'Brien

Jack Hoy

Jeff Olimpo

Jim Algeo

Jim Kunze

Jim Roos

Jim Wagner

Joe Marino

Joe Zohil

John Davis

John Kelly

John Saldutti

John Walsh

Ken Cloeren

Kent Jaggers

Larry Nackarella

Mark Wickersham

Mike Green

Mike Murphy

Mike O'Brien

Mike Trotter

Owen Collins

Pat Curley

Paul Horgan

Phil Bochey

Ralph Guiliano

Terry Trotter

Tim Love

Tom Famularo

Tom Friel

Tom Storrs

Vince Benevenuto

Managers:

Tim Dunnigan

Kevin McKelvey

Rare Breed 1978

Al Porambo

Brian Viall

Chris Hylinski

W Buzz Keough

Chris Kretschman

Charlie Murgia

Christopher Strobaugh

Donald Drakas

Danny Folkes

Frank Riffits

Gregory Kearns

H. Deskiewicz

Jim Algeo

Joe Chrismer

Jon Davis

John Henderson

John Kelly

Joseph Land

Jeffrey Mullaly

Jeffrey Olimpo

Joseph Portolese

John Saldutti

John Serafin

Jim Thompson

Jim Wagner

John Walsh

Ken Murgia

Ken Olimpo

Larry DiDomizio

Larry Nacarella

Marty Bauer

Michael Greene

Michael Murphy

Mike O'Brien

Michael Reilly

Marty Roddy

Mike Trotter

Mark Wickersham

Owen Collins

Phil Bochey

Paul Horgan

Patrick Kelly

Paul McIlhenny

R. Dyja

Ralph Guilano

Robert Haviland

Robert Heinsinger

Robert Klein

Richard Lawn

Joseph Marino

Robert McIlhenny

Rusty Ryan

Richard Saylor

Steve Kalinowski

Steve Millard

Shawn Murphy

Shawn Stratten

Tom Famularo

Thomas Friel

Timothy McNally

Thomas Storrs

Thomas Walsh

Vincent Benvenuto

Victor Lelli

William Dunn

William Shields

William Zera

Managers:

Tim Dunnigan

Kevin McKelvey

Rare Breed 1979

Al Porambo

Anthony Picozzi

Bill Dunn

Bill Shields

Bill Woebkenberg

Bob Cross

Bob Haviland

Bob Heinsinger

Bob Kelley

Bob Klein

Bob Lawn

Bob McIlhenny

Bob Williamson

Brian Lee

Brian Vile

Buz Keough

Carl Obermeier

Charlie Murgia

Chris Henderson

Chris Kane

Chris Kretchman

Chris Strobaugh

Dan Algeo

Dan Ferry

Danny Collins

Dave Jankowski

Dom Catrambone

Ed Condra

Ed Cullen

Frank Putnick

George Freeman

John Guiliano

Greg Kearns

Jeff Feulner

Jeff Olimpo

Jim Bagnell

Jim Thompson

Joe Alcott

Joe Chrismer

Joe Danko

Joe Langton

Joe Portolese

Joe Regent

John Coyle

John Delconti

John Drop

John Gorham

John Henderson

John Kelly

John Kennedy

John Mackanich

John Pedicone

John Stockmal

Jon Davis

Ken Murgia

Kevin Haviland

Larry DiDomizio

Larry Nacarella

Mark Schlegal

Mark Wickersham

Marty Roddy

Mike Bridi

Mike Klein

Mike McGinn

Mike Raber

Pat Kelly

Paul Horgan

Paul McIlhenny

Peter Walsh

Phil McIlhenny

Ralph Guiliano

Rich Lawn

Rusty Ryan

Scott Sucoloski

Shawn Smith

Steve Kalinowski

Steve Millard

Steve Ricci

Tim Kearns

Tim Kelly

Tim Viall

Tom Bagnell

Tom Casey

Tom Famularo

Tom Friel

Tom Kenney

Tom Lewandowski

Tom O'Connor

Tom Storrs

Tom Walsh

Vince Benevenuto

Wayne Davis

Managers:

Carl Arbic

Tim Dunigan

Kevin McKelvey

Rare Breed 1980

Anthony Picozzi

Bill Dunn

Bill Woebkenberg

Bob DiPasquale

Bob Haviland

Bob Klein

Bob Lawn

Bob Williamson

Brian Coyle

Brian Lawn

Brian Lee

Buzz Keough

Carl Obermeier

Chris Henderson

Chris Hylinski

Chris Kane

Chris Kardoley

Chris Strobaugh

Chuck Petrusky

Curt Fitzgerald

Dan Collins

Dan Ferry

Danny Algeo

Dave Jankowski

Dave Lawn

Dave McGaffin

Dave Steglik

David Boaman

David Bridi

Donald Blank

Don Catrambone

Ed Borkowski

Ed Condra

Ed Cullen

Frank Putnick

Greg Kearns

Jeff Feulner

Jerald Bagley

Jim Bagnell

Jim Dwyer

Jim Gotlewski

Jim Thompson

Joe Alcott

Joe Langton

Joe Portolese

Joe Rejent

John Coyle

John DelConte

John Drop

John Guiliano

John Liberto

John Mackanich

John Pedicone

Ken Murgia

Kevin Haviland

Kevin Mahoney

Larry DiDomizio

Manus McHugh

Mark Altrogge

Marty Roddy

Matt Roddy

Michael Raber

Mike Basilii

Mike Hino

Mike Klein

Mike McGinn

Mike Sodoman

Pat Kelly

Paul Malatesta

Paul McIlhenny

Peter Walsh

Rich Lawn

Robert Bell

Rob Finkelston

Ron Lutz

Rusty Ryan

Scott Sucoloski

Sean Cullen

Shawn Murphy

Shawn Pheil

Shawn Stratten

Steve Kalinowski

Steve Millard

Steve Ricci

Tim Borgmann

Tim Kearns

Tim Kelly

Tim Viall

Tom Bagnell

Tom Kenney

Tom Lewandowski

Tom Narolewski

Tom Wilson

Tony Hipple

Tony Lagreca

Wayne Davis

Manager:

Kevin McKelvey

Rare Breed 1981

Anthony Picozzi

Bill Ulwelling

Bobby Lawn

Bob DiPasquale

Bob O'Reilly

Bob Williamson

Bob Zimmerman

Brian Coyle

Brian Lawn

Brian Love

Brian O'Callaghan

Carl Obermeier

Chris Davis

Chris Henderson

Chris Kane

Dan Algeo

Dan Collins

Dan Ferry

Dave Anderson

Dave Arbic

Dave Jankowski

Dave Jungkind

Dave Leach

Dave Steglik

Dom Catrambone

Don Blank

Doug Perry

Ed Borkowski

Ed Cullen

Ed Puskoskie

Hank Farrel

Jack Hanzok

Jamie Rejent

Jeff Feulner

Jeff Kratz

Jim Bagnell

Jim Dwyer

Jim Gotlewski

Jim Honicker

Jim Hughes

Joe Alcott

Joe Drakas

Joe Langton

Joe McKenna

Joe Regent

Joe Rossi

John Bagnell

John Bereschak

John Coyle

Joe Drakas

John Drop

John Fink

John Guiliano

John Herman

John Liberto

John Mackanich

John Pedicone

John Richter

John Yaich

Keith Burrell

Ken Kociban

Kevin Haviland

Kevin Mahoney

Kurt Fitzgerald

Mark Sucoloski

Mark Teller

Marlin Raber

Mike Basilii

Mike Figlio

Mike Hino

Mike Kenney

Mike Klein

Mike Lewandowski

Mike McCarthy

Mike McGinn

Mike Murphy

Mike Totaro

Nick Fazzolari

Pat Kelly

Pat Nolan

Paul Kruzelock

Paul Malatesta

Paul McIlhenny

Pete Walsh

Piero Corrado

Sean Cliver

Ray Mease

Rich Stead

Rick Carrasco

Rob Bell

Rob Finkelston

Ron Lutz

Scott Sucoloski

Sean Cullen

Sean Cliver

Sol Honicker

Steve Paillard

Steve Roddy

Tim Borgman

Tim Irvin

Tim Kearns

Tom Bagnell

Tom Casey

Tom Kenny

Tom Lewandowski

Tom Narowleski

Tom O'Connor

Tony LaGreca

Tony Sandone

Wayne Davis

Rare Breed 1982

Anthony Picozzi

Bob DiPasquale

Bob Williamson

Carl Obermeier

Chris Davis

Chris Henderson

Chris Walsh

Curt Fitzgerald

Dan Collins

Dave Leach

Dave Steglik

Dan Algeo

Don Blank

Doug Perry

Ed Borkowski

Ed Puskoski

Jack Honzak

Jamie Rejent

Jeff Kratz

Jim Bagnell

Jim Gotlewski

Jim Honniker

Joe Drakas

Joe Mckenna

Joe Regent

Joe Rossi

John Bagnell

John Coyle

John Drop

John Richter

Ken Kociban

Kevin Mahoney

Mark Sucoloski

Matt Krier

Mike Figlio

Mike Hino

Mike Klein

Mike Lewandowski

Mike Murphy

Mike Totaro

Pat Nolan

Paul Malatesta

Rich Steg

Ron Lutz

Scott Sucoloski

Sean Cliver

Sol Honniker

Steve Ricci

Steve Roddy

Tim Borgman

Tom Lewandowski

Tom Narolewski

Tom O'Connor

Tony LeGreca

Tony Sandone

Rare Breed 1983

Andrew Blank

Bill Pepper

Bob Busfield

Bob Drakas

Bob Minnucci

Brian St. Clair

Chris Bank

Chris Davis

Chris McDemus

Chris Walsh

Curt Fitzgerald

Dan Cardamone

Daniel Porambo

Dave Lawn

Dave Leach

Dave Steglik

Den Blank

Doug Perry

Ed Borkowski

Ed Obermier

Ed Puskowskie

Erik Chesla

Frank Haley

Gary Drakas

Gerald Collins

Greg Cheney

J. Boreschak

James Curran

James LeGates

James McCarthy

Vincent Bringenberg

James Neve

Jamie Rejent

Jason Borkowski

Jeff Kratz

Jeffrey Glueck

Jim Honicker

Joe Drakas

Joe Guiliano

Joe Kuhn

Joe Rossi

John Bagnell

John Herman

John Richter

John Yaich

Joseph Burns

Joseph Karwoski

Joseph Loughran

Joseph Schwab

Kevin Mahoney

Ken Kociban

Kevin Deetz

Mark Sucoloski

Martin Grourke

Michael Harrington

Michael Koder

Michael Marino

Mike Drop

Mike Figlio

Mike Hino

Mike Lewandowski

Mike Murphy

Mike Totaro

Mike Wagner

Pat Nolan

Paul Malatesta

Paul Moretski

Pete Grubb

Phil Baney

Raymond Liberto

Timothy Trotter

Remo DiFrancesco

Rich Hart

Rick Coughlin

Rick Stead

Rick Williams

Robert Culp

Rob Zimmerman

Ron Lutz

Scott Hallman

Sean Cliver

Shawn Friel

Steve Adams

Steve Killian

Steve Roddy

Tim Borgmann

Tim Irvin

Tom Narolewski

Tony LaGreca

Tony Sandone

Tony Serafino

William Benedict

Rare Breed 1984

Alan Jarvis

Andy Myers

Benny Poccia

Bob Culp

Brendan Kowlaczyk

Brendan Sweeney

Brian Fahey

Chris Banko

Chris Walsh

Chuck LaMelza

Dan Parambo

Dave Adams

Dave Drop

Dave Leach

Dave Millard

Dominic Vangelli

Don German

Doug Perry

Eric Ferrerri

Eric Scheetz

John Tumelty

John Storri

John Cullen

Jamie Rejent

Jay Garron

Jon Dembrosky

Greg Cheney

Jamie Kratz

Jamie Rejent

Jamie Taylor

Jay Borkowski

Jeff Kratz

Jim Curran

Jim Honicker

Jim Neve

Jim Pepper

Joe Burns

Joe Bifolco

Joe Rossi

John Richter

John Bagnell

Tony Sandone

John Richter

Karl Zimmerman

Keith Fryslin

Keith Hallman

M.J. Grourke

Matt Chesla

Mark Migliaccio

Mike Chermela

Mike Fink

Mike Murphy

Mike Picozzi

Mike Totaro

Mike Wagner

Pat Dougherty

Pat McOwen

Pat Nolan

Pete Grubb

Phil Baney

Ray Liberto

Remo DiFrancesco

Rob Zimmerman

Shawn Friel

Shawn Malloy

Shawn Friel

Steve Adams

Steve Conduit

Steve Roddy

Tim Leach

Tim Trotter

Tom Borkowski

Rare Breed 1985

Brendan Sweeney

Brian Corrado

Ben DeMonte

Brian Friel

Billy Knapp

Bob Culp

Brian Grubb

Chuck Lamelza

Chris Malatesta

Christopher Walsh

Daniel Cardamone

Shawn Friel

Dan Drop

D. Lynch

Dan Porambo

Douglas Cordero

Eric Ferretti

Eric Sheetz

Greg Cheney

Gregory Ferraro

Greg Mitsch

Sean Greene

Henry Nolan

Hank Sikorski

Joseph Burns

John Cullen

Jon Dembrowsky

John Eadeh

Joe Falco

John Gotlewski

Joe Guiliano

John Gunder

J. Heart

James Kratz

Joe Kuhn

James Lelii

Jeffrey Mullin

Jim Neve

James Pepper

John Pelna

John Storti

James Taylor

Keith Hallman

Karl Zimmerman

Jay Borkowski

Mike Chermela

Matt Chesla

Mike Coughlin

Mike Drop

Mike Greer

M.J. Grourke

Mike Kuhn

Michael Marino

Mark McNutt

Mark Migliaccio

Tim Leach

Michael Parante

Michael Picozzi

Mike Wagner

Peter Grubb

P. J. Kang

Remo DiFrancesco

Steve Adams

Ray Liberto

Sean Fitzsimmons

K. O'Brien

Steve Killian

Shawn Malloy

Sean St. Clair

Tom Borkowski

Tim Cooper

Tom Filanowicz

Tim Trotter

Tony Ventresca

Tony Yankowski

Victor Ykoruk

Rare Breed 1986

Bob Coons

Bob Culp

Brian Friel

Bill Knapp

Brian St. Clair

Brendan Sweeney

Chuck Lamelza

Chris Ryan

Doug Cordero

Dan Drop

Dan Porambo

Eric Ferretti

Erik Scheetz

Greg Ferraro

Greg Mitsch

Henry Nolan

Jay Borkowski

Joe Burns

Jon Dembrowski

Joe Falco

John Gotlewski

James Kratz

James Lelii

Jeffrey Mullin

Jim Neve

John Pelna

J. Reichert

John Storti

James Taylor

Keith Hallman

K. O'Brien

Karl Zimmerman

Michael Anthony

Michael Chermela

Matt Chesla

M.J. Grourke

Michael Kuhn

Michael Marino

Mark McNutt

Mark Migliaccio

Mike Picozzi

Peter Grubb

Ray Liberto

Sean Greene

Tim Cooper

Tim Leach

Tony Rezza

Tim Trotter

Thomas Weiderman

Rare Breed 1987

Anthony DiDonato

Bill Knapp

Brendan Sweeney

Brent Schaffer

Brian Friel

Brian Grubb

Chris Bair

Chris Malatesta

Chris Ryan

Chuck Lamelza

Dan Drop

Ken O'Brien

Dan Myers

Dave Drop

Dave Mills

Eric Ferretti

Frank Rezza

Hank Nolan

Fred Holdsworth

George Haldeman

Greg Ferraro

Greg Mitsch

Jamie Kratz

Jason Glemser

Jim Calafati

Jim Kearney

Jim Lelii

Jim Taylor

Joe Calafati

Joe Falco

Joe Maule

Joe Roos

John Gotlewski

John Pelna

Keith Hallman

John Storti

John Strauss

Jon Dembrosky

Jon Kratz

Karl Zimmerman

Mark McNutt

Mike Chermela

Mike Kuhn

Mike Picozzi

Mike Rieg

Mike Steelman

Noell Maerz

Pete Kane

Phil Braccio

Rob Pecharo

Sean St. Clair

Seung Lee

Shawn Malloy

Tim Cooper

Tim Leach

Tony Herzog

Tony Rezza

Rare Breed 1988

Bill Knapp

Bob Scott

Brent Schaffer

Brian Friel

Brian Grubb

Brian Orsino

Chris Ambolino

Chris Bair

Chris Malatesta

Chris Ryan

Dan Drop

Dave DeHaven

Dave Mills

Frank Buchy

Frank Radomski

Frank Wrubel

George Haldeman

Greg Ferraro

Greg Mitsch

Hank Nolan

Jason Chermela

Jason Hazzard

Jim Calafati

Jim Lelii

Joe Calafati

Joe Falco

Joe Maule

Joe Roos

Joe Schulz

Joe Speece

John Falco

John Gotlewski

John Pelna

John Strauss

Jon Kratz

Kevin McCullagh

Keith McCullagh

Lou Calvanese

Mark McNutt

Matt Hendricks

Mike Calafati

Mike Gozzard

Mike Kuhn

Mike Rieg

Noell Maerz

Pat Burns

Pete Kane

Rob Pecharo

Ron Wolfe

Seung Lee

Thomas McNutt

Tim Cooper

Tony Rezza

Rare Breed 1989

Bill Doughty

Bob Scott

Brent Schaffer

Chris Ambolino

Chris Bair

Chris Cossman

Chris Fanelli

Chris O'Reilly

Chris Ployd

Chris Trumbore

Chris Vinal

Chris Wagner

Chuck Diener

Dan Carr

Dave Ateek

Dave DeHaven

Dave Delciotto

Dave Mills

Ed Quinn

Elvio DiCarlantonio

Erich Maerz

Frank Buchy

Frank Radomski

George Haldeman

Jason Chermela

Jason Glemser

Jason Hazzard

Jim Calafati

Joe Calafati

Joe Maule

Joe Roos

Joe Schulz

John Hutchinson

John Strauss

Jon Feulner

Kevin McCullagh

Keith McCullagh

Mark Kramer

Matt Coletta

Matt Dempsey

Mike Angelo

Mike Calafati

Mike Cliver

Mike Gozzard

Mike Mattero

Mike Rieg

Mike Steelman

Noel Maerz

Pete Kane

Richie O'Neill

Ron Wolfe

Sean Williams

Seung Lee

Steve DiGiuseppe

Thom McNutt

Tim Kiely

Tom Zecca

Rare Breed 1990

Andy Schulz

Anthony Ciccocelli

Bill Doughty

Bob Scott

Brendan Kelly

Chris Ambolino

Chris Cossman

Chris Fanelli

Chris Higham

Chris Keegan

Chris Ployd

Chris Trumbore

Chuck Diener

Cliff Motley

Dan Carr

Dan Richards

Dave DeHaven

Dave Delciotto

Dave Miller

Ed Quinn

Elvio DiCariantonio

Erich Maerz

Frank Foye

Frank Radamski

Greg Colelli

Greg Webb

Guy Dougherty

Jason Chermela

Jason Hazzard

Jeff Gunder

Jeff Primus

Jim Calafati

Joel Greco

Joe McGinley

Joe Schulz

Joe Trave

John Hutchinson

Jon Feulner

Kevin McCullagh

Keith McCullagh

Kris Kita

Mark Kramer

Martin Early

Matt Battista

Matt Dempsey

Matt Schwartz

Mike Angelo

Mike Calafati

Mike Garner

Mike Gozzard

Nick Calafati

Richie O'Neill

Ron Plummer

Sam Veneziale

Sean Quigley

Sean Williams

Steve DiGiuseppe

Steve Gonczkowski

Tom Brown

Tom Zecca

Rare Breed 1991

Andy Schulz

B.J. Gothier

Bill Doughty

Brian Benner

Brian Beno

Chris Claffey

Chris Cossman

Chris Fanelli

Chris Hartman

Chris Higham

Chris Ployd

Chris Trumbore

Chuck Diener

Cliff Motley

Dan Richards

Dave Delciotto

Dave Dembrosky

Ed Quinn

Elvio DiCarlantonio

Erich Maerz

Frank Buchy

Frank Foye

Greg Fitzsimmons

Guy Dougherty

Hector Roman

Jeff Custer

Jeff Gunder

Joe Trave

John Hutchinson

John Woehlcke

Jon Feulner

Justin Strauss

Ken Thorpe

Mark Kramer

Martin Earley

Matt Fallon

Matt Schwartz

Mike Bender

Mike Dungan

Mike Dynan

Mike Garner

Mike Grondalski

Mike Krapf

Nick Calafati

Pat Roddy

Rich Homolash

Rich O'Neill

Ron Plummer

Ryan Hendel

Sean Quigley

Tom Baney

Tom Brown

Tom Homolash

Vince Ball

Rare Breed 1992

Andy Schulz

Chris Hartman

Cliff Motley

Dan Richards

Doug Thorpe

Eric Gozzard

Frank Foye

Gary Calafati

Greg Fitzsimmons

Guy Dougherty

Jeff Custer

Jeff Gunder

Jeff Kuntz

Joe McAteer

Joe Neve

Joe Trave

John Pasquella

John Woehlcke

Justin Strauss

Ken Thorpe

Kevin Friel

Luke Moyer

Mark Chesla

Martin Earley

Matt Kramer

Matt Schwartz

Mike Bender

Mike Dungan

Mike Dynan

Mike Garner

Mike Neubert

Nick Calafati

Patrick Roddy

Ralph Calafati

Dave Dembrosky

Rob McMaster

Ron Plummer

Ross Setaro

Ryan Hendel

Scott Gardner

Sean Quigley

Steve Gonczkowski

Steve Parente

Tim Quinn

Tom Baney

Tom Brown

Rare Breed 1993

Archie Allen

Bryan Parente

Chris Hartman

Dave Colletti

Dave Dembrosky

Dan Shallow

Dennis Szymanski

Doug Thorpe

Eric Gozzard

Gary Calafati

Greg Fitzsimmons

Hector Roman

James Chavous

Joe Colella

Joe McAteer

Jeff Custer

Justin Strauss

John Woehlcke

John Algeo

Kevin Carney

Kevin Cope

Kevin Friel

Ken Thorpe

Kevin Tisdale

Mark Chesla

Mike Deviney

Mike Dungan

Michael Dynan

Mark Tavani

Matt Kramer

Michael Murphy

Mike Oberholtzer

Matt Bender

Mike Bender

Neil Greene

Patrick Kelly

Patrick Roddy

Ryan Bodman

Rob McMaster

Rob Carickhoff

Ryan McCarthy

Sean Buchy

Scott Garner

Stephen Lewis

Stephen Parente

Stephen Pasquini

Tom Baney

Tim Quinn

Rare Breed 1994

Adam Ziegler

Anthony Greene

Bryan Parente

Chris Walsh

Curt Johnston

Dave Colletti

Dennis White

Eric Gozzard

Gary Calafati

Greg Kozminski

Jamey Corrigan

Jeff DiVicaris

Jim O'Connor

Joe Colella

Joe McAteer

John Algeo

John Arent

Josh Woodward

Kevin Friel

Kevin Tisdale

Leo Horscher

Luke Moyer

Mark Strauss

Mark Tavani

Mark Weber

Matt Bender

Mike deMarteleire

Mike McGinley

Mike Oberholtzer

Neil Greene

Nick Hoover

Rich Riccio

Rob Carickhoff

Rob Lombardo

Rob McMaster

Rocco Rossini

Ryan McCarthy

Scott Garner

Sean Buchy

Steve Berardi

Steve Lewis

Tim Quinn

Tim Seiders

Rare Breed 1995

Alfred Panico

Andrew Trumbore

Andy Dziedzic

Brad Stephan

Brian Foye

Chris Miller

Chris Walsh

Chuck Clemente

Curt Johnston

Dave Colletti

Dave Outland

Dennis White

Eric Lukens

Frank Panzullo

Greg Kozminski

Jamie Corrigan

Jeff DeVicaris

Joe Colella

Joe Keating

Joe Rissi

John Algeo

John Arent
Josh Woodward
Ken Kozminski
Kevin Boyle
Kevin Tisdale
Mark Cianchetta
Mark Strauss
Mark Tavani
Matt Bender
Matt Naldzin
Mike DeFilippo
Mike deMarteleire
Mike Fitzsimmons
Mike McGinley
Mike Nowakowski
Mike Oberholtzer
Mike Wynne
Neil Greene
Nick Hoover
Paul Falco
Rich Riccio
Rob Carickhoff
Rob DeFinis
Rob Lombardo
Ryan McCarthy
Sean Buchy
Steve Bender
Steve Berardi
Tae Woo
Tim Hermann
Tim Seiders

Rare Breed 1996

Andrew Potson

Andrew Ratke

Andrew Santacroce

Andrew Trumbore

Bill Fisher

Brian Foye

Brian Geiger

Brian Koch

Dave Outland

Brian Shields

Brian Smith

Bryan McGee-Skinner

Bryan McSherry

Chip Panico

Chris Balwin

Chris Miller

Chuck Clemente

Dave Belfatti

Curt Johnston

Dan McGarry

Dan Monoghan

Dave Befatti

Dave Outland

Dennis White

Drew Bardissi

Frank Panzullo

Greg Kozminski

J. R. McCabe

Jack Byers

Jamie Corrigan

Jeff DeVicario

Jeffrey Fink

Jim Geuke

Jim McCarthy

Joe Cianchetta

Joe Keating

Joe Rissi

John Arent

John Bryner

John Turner

John Walsh

Joseph Judge

Joseph Kellogg

Joseph Saldutti

Ken Kozminski

Kenneth Baumbach

Kevin Boyle

Kevin Moloney

Liam Larkin

Mark Brunner

Mark Cianchetta

Mark Neimeister

Matt McShea

Matt Stairiker,

Michael McCosker

Mike Cianchetta

Mike De Filippo

Mike deMarteleire, Jr.

Mike Fitzsimmons

Mike McGinley

Mike Nowakowski

Nick Bilyk

Nick Hoover

Paul Falco

Rich Riccio

Rob DeFinis

Robert Pritchard

Rob Lombardo

Ryan Moloney

Chris Smith

Scott Byers

Scott Coughlin

Scott Sikorski

Scott Tisdale

Sean Stephan

Shaun Lewis

Shon Grosse

Steve Bender

Steve Berardi

Steve DeSteffano

Steve Jones

Tae Woo

Thomas Mitchell

Tim Hermann

Tim Moyer

Tim Seiders

Wayne Volpe

William Andreoni

Rare Breed 1997

Andrew Potson

Andrew Ratke

Andrew Trumbore

Bill Andreoni

Bill Fischer

Brian Foye

Brian Geiger

Brian Shields

Bryan Magee-Skinner

Chip Panico

Chris Miller

Chris Quinn

Chuck Clemente

Dave Belfatti

Ed McAlanis

Frank Panzullo

J. R. McCabe

Jack Byers

Jim Geueke

Jim McCarthy

Joe Judge

Joe Keating

Joe Kellogg

Joe Rissi

John Bryner

John Coughlin

John Walsh

Jon Hassinger

Ken Kozminski

Kevin Bonner

Kevin Boyle

Kevin Moloney

Kevin Ryan

Liam Larkin

Mark Brunner

Mark Cianchetta

Matt McShea

Matt Stairiker

Michael DeFilippo

Michael McCosker

Michael McGinley

Mike deMarteleire

Mike Fitzsimmons

Mike Nowakowski

Rob DeFinis

Ryan Moloney

Scott Keating

Scott Sikorski

Shaun Lewis

Steve Bender

Steve DeSteffano

Tim Hermann

Tim Moyer

Tom Mitchell

Wayne Volpe

Rare Breed 1998

Allen Andracavage

Bill Andreoni

Bill Farina

Brian Fitzsimmons

Brian Campbell

Brian Geiger

Brian Hermann

Brian Shields

Bryan Magee-Skinner

Chip Panico

Chris Quinn

Dave Belfatti

Dave Rausch

Drew Bardissi

Greg Gaffney

Greg Schratz

Jack Byers

Jim Geueke

Jim McCarthy

Jim O'Hara

Jim Roddy

Joe Judge

Joe Kellogg

Joe Palmerio

John Bryner

John Coughlin

John Walsh

Kevin Bonner

Kevin Iredale

Kevin Keating

Kevin Moloney

Kevin Ryan

Mark Brunner

Mark Roscilo

Matt Stairiker

Mike Agnew

Mike McAteer

Mike McCosker

Nick Vollman

Ryan Moloney

Ryan Witt

Scott Keating

Scott Sikorski

Sean Kroszner

Sean Trotter

Shaun Lewis

Steve Mocey

Tim Marrer

Tim Moyer

Will Mooney

Rare Breed 1999

A.J. Kennedy

Andrew Nave

Bill Andreoni

Brian Hermann

Bryan Magee-Skinner

Dave Rausch

Greg Gaffney

Jason Phifer

Jason St. Onge

Jay Moon

Jeff Watts

Jim Roddy

Joe Judge

Joe Kellogg

Joe Palmerio

Joe White

John Coughlin

Jon Steever

Justin Johnston

Kevin Iredale

Kevin Keating

Mike Agnew

Mike Bennicelli

Mike Fanelli

Mike Galla

Mike McAteer

Mike McCosker

Mike Sykes

Nick Vollman

Patrick Fitzsimmons

Ryan Moloney

Scott Keating

Sean Kroszner

Sean Trotter

Shaun Lewis

Steve Magerl

Steve Mocey

Terry Mulvey

Tim Dunn

Tim Marrer

Tim Moyer

Tim Paul

Tim Stairiker

Will Mooney

Rare Breed 2000

A. J. Kennedy

Adam Corrado

Anthony Byers

Bill Kelly

Brandon Grosso

Brian Fitzsimmons

Brian Herman

Chase Hagan

Chris McCarty

Chris Meyer

Chris Schoenberger

Chuck Grohoski

Dan Cornell

Dave Rausch

Dave Thomas

Greg Gaffney

Jeff Watts

Jim Roddy

Jon Steever

Justin Grohoski

Justin Johnston

Kevin Iredale

Kevin Keating

Mario Ventresca

Kyle Kroszner

Mark Cannon

Mark Roscilo

Matt Riley

Mike Bennicelli

Mike Donahue

Mike Fanelli

Mike McAteer

Mike Sykes

Nick Vollman

Paul Koch

Scott Keating

Sean Kroszner

Sean Trotter

Jason St. Onge

Steve Magerl

Steve Mocey

Tim Dunn

Tim Marrer

Tim Paul

Tim Stairiker

Vince Scaramuzza

Vince Tucciarone

Will Mooney

Rare Breed 2001

Anthony Byers

Anthony Celona

Adam Corrado

Anthony Fucinari

A.J. Kennedy

Brendan Brett

Brian Cottone

Brendan Fitzsimmons

Brian Folkes

Brandon Grosso

Bill Kelly

B. Strauss

Brendan Woodward

Christopher Antoni

Christopher Donahue

Chuck Grohoski

Chase Hagan

Chris Meyer

Chris Schoenberger

C. Siso

C. Tarlecki

Chris Vosoli

Dan Espada

Dave Lomas

E. Mercer

E. Otto

Eric Quinn

E. Seeger

J. Atkins

Jason Gilles

Justin Grohoski

Justin Johnston

Ji Mon Kwon

Jim Mariano

Jesse Miele

J. Romeo

Jason St. Onge

Jeff Watts

Kevin Byers

Kyle Dunn

K. Grady

Kevin Keating

Kyle Kroszner

M. Beniccelli

Mark Cannon

M. Cantrell

Mike Donahue

M. Gwynn

Mitch Kulp

Michael McKay

Matt Moneta

Mike Sykes

Mario Ventresca

Michael Wasylenko

Nate Kraynak

Phillip Deis

P. Reiff

Paul Wagenhoffer

Rob Boccuti

R.C. Lagomarsino

R. Maycourt

Rob Trier

Bob Walsh

Steven Edling

Shaun MacMinn

Scott Ryan

Timothy Donahue

Tim Dunn

T. Matteo

Tim Stairiker

V. Tucciarone

Walter Rada

Rare Breed 2002

Adam Corrado

Anthony Byers

Billy Kelly

Bob Walsh

Brendan Brett

Brendan Fitzsimmons

Brendan Woodward

Brian Cottone

Brian Folkes

Brian Madden

Chase Hagan

Chris Antoni

Chris Meyer

Chris Schoenberger

Chris Vasoli

Dan Espada

Dan Kunze

Dave Lomas

Eric Quinn

Ji Min Kwon

Jim Mariano

John Bergandino

Justin Grohoski

Kevin Byers

Kyle Kroszner

Mario Ventresca

Mark Cannon

Matt Moneta

Mike Adams

Mike Donahue

Mitch Kulp

Nate Kraynak

Nick Menzen

Patrick Lewis

Paul Wagonhoffer

R. C. Lagomarsino

Rickey Ventresca

Rob Boccuti

Rob Trier

Ron Macort

Ron Waskiewicz

Ryan Pasko

Scott Ryan

Vinnie Tucciarone

Rare Breed 2003

Andrew Hill

Brendan Brett

Brian Cottone

Brendan Hartman

Ben Morano

Bob Walsh

Christopher Antoni

Craig Pluto

Chris Vasoli

David Butler

Daniel Kunze

Drew Lagomarsino

David Lomas

Dan Espada

Dan Kroszner

Dylan Saldutti

Eric Quinn

J. Gibson

Jim Marino

Jake Watts

Mike Adams

Michael Craig

Mitch Kulp

Mike Opdyke

Michael Unger

Matt Moneta

Nate Kraynak

N. Mensen

Patrick Lewis

Paul Wagenhoffer

Robert Boccuti

R.C. Lagomarsino

Ronald Macort

Ryan Pasko

Ryan Sexton

Rob Trier

Scott Hills

Scott Ryan

Sal Nocchi

Sean Kirk

Thomas Folkes

Tom Kelly

Thomas Malecki

V. Binnacle

Rare Breed 2004

Anthony Bennicelli

Ben Morano

Bob Ryan

Bob Walsh

Brendan Brett

Brendan Fitzsimmons

Brian Cottone

Chris Vasoli

Craig Pluta

Dan Espada

Dan Kroszner

Dan Smith

Dave Woods

Drew Lagomarsino

Dylan Saldutti

Eric Quinn

Greg Walsh

Ian Davis

Jake Watts

Jim Charpentier

Jim Flanigan

Jim Kelly

Jim Mariano

Joe Pirner

John Nelligan

Josh Homa

Kevin Bolton

Matt Moneta

Mike Adams

Mike Craig

Mike Opdyke

Mike Swain

Nate Kraynak

Patrick Lewis

R.C. Lagomarsino

Ryan Sexton

Sal Nocchi

Scott Hills

Sean Kirk

Sean Pfeiffer

Tom Kelly

Tom Malecki

Vic Bennicelli

Rare Breed 2005

Steve Barr

Victor Bennicelli

Kevin Bolton

Will Bray

Joe Budka

Dave Butler

Lloyd Caspter

Jim Charpentier

Ian Davis

Rob Day

Andrew Hill

Scott Hills

Josh Homa

Jared Homa

Rick Hummel

Jim Kelly

Tom Kelly

Sean Kirk

Dan Kroszner

Pete Krozner

Drew Lagomarsino

Patrick Lewis

Tom Malecki

Rocky Mariano

James Moloney

Ben Morano

Gino Moscariello

John Nelligan

Sal Nocchi

Mike Opdyke

Sean Pfeiffer

Shane Pinzka

Joe Pimer

Craig Pluta

Bob Ryan

Dylan Saldutti

Mike Selby

Ryan Sexton

Dan Smith

Mike Swain

Donato Tumulo

Greg Wash

Jake Watts

Sean Wojdula

Rare Breed 2006

Alec Bonacci

Andrew Hill

Andrew Keyes

Andrew Mims

Bob Fisher

Bob Ryan

Brendan Wood

Brian Keane

Brian Mocey

Chris Nodecker

Dan Frantz

Dan Smith

Donato Tumulo

Gennaro Capone

Gino Moscariello

Greg Walsh

Gus Feleccia

James Moloney

Jess Fields

Jim Charpentier

Jim Kelly

Joe Hogan

John Howell

John Nelligan

Kevin Bolton

Kevin Miller

Kyle Davis

Matt Kirby

Matt Pluta

Mickey Kahrs

Mike Curry

Mike Selby

Neil Cabellero

Pete Kroszner

Peter Kenworthy

Rick Hummel

Rob Day

Rocky Mariano

Ryan Tiedeman

Sean Kelly

Sean Pfeiffer

Sean Wojdula

Shane Pinzka

Steve Barr

Will Bray

Rare Breed 2007

Adam Wrigley

Alec Bonacci

Alex Hetzel

John Howell

Bobby O'Connor

Bob Fisher

Brandon Lewandowski

Brian Wisman

Chris Nodecker

Dan Plummer

Devon Barrett

Ethan Barrett

Gino Moscarieillo

Gus Feleccia

James Moloney

Jim Kelly

Jim Moser, Jim

John Bruno-Costanzo

Kevin McGinn

Kevin Miller

Mali Pluta

Matt McGouldrick

Mickey Kahrs

Mike Curry

Mike Selby

Neil Caballero

Nick Manai

Patrick O'Hara

Pete Kenworthy

Pete Kroszner

Ricky Ronan

Rocky Mariano

Ryan Tiedeman

Sam Kraynak

Sean Kelly

Sean Wojdula

Shane Pinzka

Steve Barr

Steve Day

Tom Gaus

Tom Glenn

Will Bray

Rare Breed 2008

Adam Moczydlowski

Alec Bonacci

Alex Hetzel

Andrew Mandato

Bobby O'Connor

Bob Fisher

Brandon Lewandowski

Brian Wisman

Chris Bray

Chris Nodecker

Cody Smykal

Dan Plummer

Dennis Hoyer

Chuck Karr

Devon Barrett

Ethan Barrett

Jim Moser

Joe Ward

John Bruno-Constanzo

John Derosier

John Howell

John Welch

Kevin Fitzpatrick

Kevin Geueke

Kevin McGinn

Kevin Miller

Louis Manai

Matt Goldstein

Matt McGouldrick

Matt Pluta

Matt Wallace

Mike Bradley

Mike Curry

Mike Serratore

Nick Manai

Nick Seaton

Patrick O'Hara

Matt Pinzka

Pete Kenworthy

Quinn Martin

Rich Trotter

Rich Walsh

Ricky Ronan

Ryan Tiedeman

Sean Kelly

Sean MacGuire

Steve Day

Tim Nelligan

Tom Cleary

Tom Gaus

Tom Shields

Will Schoener

Rare Breed 2009

Alex Hetzel

Andrew Mandato

Andrew Slavin

Brian Wisman

Chris Casper

Colin Borusiewicz

Dan Kees

Dan Pederson

Dan Plummer

Dennis Hoyer

Joe Kaiser

Devon Barrett

Evan Coughlin

Gabe Palmerio

Jim Moser

Jim Nelligan

Joe Leddy

Joe Lee

Joe Ward

John Bruno-Costanzo

John Derosier

John Welch

Kevin Cox

Kevin Fitzpatrick

Kevin Geueke

Kevin McGinn

Matt Goldstein

Matt McGouldrick

Matt McNamee

Matt Pinzka

Matt Shenko

Matt Wallace

Mike Bradley

Mike Larson

Mike Malecki

Mike Serratore

Nick Seaton

Patrick O'Hara

Pat Schoenberger

Quinn Martin

Richard Walsh

Ryan Tiedeman

Scott Catalano

Sean Maguire

Steve Day

Steve Newell

Tim Fitzpatrick

Tom Gaus

Tom Shields

Tyler Smith

Rare Breed 2010

Adam Zawadzki

Alex Hetzel

Alex Schneidinger

Andrew Mandato

Anthony Foraker

Austin Bauersmith

Brian Casey

Brian Rafferty

Charles Martin

Chris Casper

Corey Kirk

Dan Pederson

Darryl Saylor

Den Hover

Devon Barrett

Dillon Algeo

Dominic Moscariello

Dylan Kinee

Evan Coughlin

Evan Dehaven

Jack Shields

James Ward

Jimmy Marr

Joe Jefferson

Joe Shmid

Joe Ward

John DeRosier

Jude Coughlin

Justin Angco

Justin Cook

Kevin Fitzpatrick

Kevin Geueke

Kevin Sabo

Kyle Ramsay

Ian Bates

Mike Larson

Mark Welch

Mason Schmauder

Matt Goldstein

Matt Pinzka

Matt Shenko

Matt Wallace

Max Wengyn

Mike Bradley

Mike Jester

Mike Iacono

Mike Larson

Mike Malecki

Mike Serratore

Nick Albanese

Nick Cardillo

Nick Seaton

Pat Duggan

Pat Hill

Patrick Duggan

Pat Schoenberger

Paul Northrop

Phil Seger

Quinn Martin

Rich Walsh

Ryan Gianoni

Scott Catalano

Shane Schmauder

Steve Newell

Steve Snider

Thomas Moczydlowski

Tim Fitzpatrick

Tom Gibbons

Tom Shields

Tyler Smith

Tyler Viers

Zach Talley

Rare Breed 2011

Andrew McClintock

Brian Casee

Chris Sniscak

Dan Pedersen

Dillon Algeo

Ed Mckee

Evan Coughlin

Evan DeHaven

Ian Bates

Ian Fischetti

Jack Shields

Jake Clauss

James Basile

James Ward

Jim Cassady

Joe Pinzka

Joe Schmidt

John Kweder

John Sagl

Jude Coughlin

Justin Gaumer

Karl Brill

Kevin Sabo

Kevin Salfi

Mason Schmauder

Matt Plummer

Max Wengyn

Mike Iacono

Mike Jester

Mike Larson

Mike Malecki

Nick Albanese

Nick Cardillo

Pat Farris

Patrick Duggan

Pat Schoenberger

Reece Hoyer

Ryan Gianoni

Sean Mills

Shane Schmauder

Steve Snyder

Tim Duggan

Tim Fitzpatrick

Tom Antenucci

Tom Gibbons

Tyler Smith

Tyler Viers

Zach Talley

Credits and Acknowledgments

The Lansdale Historical Society has graciously provided access to Lansdale Catholic High School Yearbooks, as well to *The North Penn Reporter*.

President Kennedy's public domain remarks on the sea from *"Remarks in Newport at the Australian Ambassador's Dinner for the America's Cup Crews (383),"* September 14, 1962, *Public Papers of the Presidents: John F. Kennedy, 1962*.

Vince Lombardi quotes used with permission by the Family of Vince Lombardi, www.VinceLombardi.com. All rights reserved.

A special thanks to the many Lansdale Catholic community members who interviewed, sent written contributions, or offered invaluable guidance:

James Algeo, Sr.

Mary Margaret Algeo

Uncle Michael Algeo

Aunt Eileen Algeo

Aunt Sally Filliben

Aunt Mary Freburger

Maggie deMarteleire, LC Class of 1978

Michael deMarteleire, Sr., LC Assistant Coach

Mike Wagner, LC Class of 1986

Joe Wengyn, LC Parent Classes 2014 and 2018

Chet Wisniewski, LC Class of 1969

Patrick O'Hara, Sr. LC Class of 1970

Patrick O'Hara, Jr. LC Class of 2009

Dan Shallow, LC Assistant Coach

Anthony Sandone, Sr. LC Class of 1964 and Assistant Coach

Anthony Sandone, Jr. LC Class of 1985

John Wagner, LC Class of 1973 and Assistant Coach

Joe Ritinski, LC Class of 1973 and Assistant Coach

Richard Trotter, LC Class of 1973

Michael Gildea, LC Class of 1973

Kevin McCullagh, LC Class of 1991

Robert Culp, LC Class of 1987

Ray Lagomarsino, LC Assistant Coach

R.C. Lagomarsino, LC Class of 2005

Drew Lagomarsino, LC Class of 2006

Tom Smallwood, NP Knight, Class of 1991

Michelle Fenstermacher, LC Parent 2014 and 2015

William Bray, LC Class of 2008

Paul Lepre, LC Assistant Coach

Morgan Lepre, LC Water Specialist

Marty Roddy, LC Class of 1981

Brian Cottone, LC Class of 2005

Mike Wisniewski, LC Class of 1973

Bob Gillies, LC Class of 1978

Liz and Marty Grourke, LC Parents 1985, 1987, and 1988

David Dembrosky, LC Class of 1994

Ron and Mary Rogozinski, Class of 1965

Paul Collins, LC Class of 1976

Trish O'Callaghan Reger, LC Class of 1983

Raymond Teller, LC Class of 1983

David Leach, LC Class of 1985

Charles Murgia, LC Class of 1980

John Woehlcke, LC Class of 1994

James Kelly, LC Class of 2008

Sources

For information regarding Knute Rockne:

https://www.britannica.com/biography/Knute-Rockne

http://www.espn.com/blog/notre-dame-football/post/_/id/7403/ numbers-dont-tell-story-of-rockne

For information regarding "Four Green Fields:"
https://www.nytimes.com/2007/08/03/world/europe/03iht-03makem-globe.6972124.html

For information regarding Monsignor Joseph Schade:
https://www.lcalumni.com/history.htm

For information regarding Conrad Weiser:
http://www.conradweiserhomestead.org/

For information regarding Milton Hershey
https://www.hersheypa.com/about-hershey/history/

For information regarding Cardinal John O'Hara
https://ethicscenter.nd.edu/about/inspire/great-figures/ john-cardinal-ohara-1888-1960/

For information regarding Coach Chris Bockrath:
https://www.timesherald.com/sports/community-honors-the-memo-ry-of-chris-bockrath-inducted-into-montgomery/article_5f92950a-986e-5f4a-a263-72da854819a4.html
http://articles.mcall.com/1997-02-08/ sports/3133737_1_team-s-chances-high-school-coaching-career-league-titles

For information on Thomas Cahill:

http://irishedition.com/2016/01/1930/ Hand, Pete.
125 Years Later Roman Catholic High School Expands Thomas E.
Cahills' Dream.

For information regarding the 1998 ESPY Award:
https://www.espn.com/espy2000/s/pastwinners.html

For various events in history:
www.peoplehistory.com

Rare Breed Connections

For more information about the Rare Breed, including memories and upcoming projects, you are invited to visit the following online sites:

www.rarebreednationllc.org
Rare Breed Nation LLC Facebook Page
Football Family: Home of the Rare Breed YouTube
Lansdale Catholic Football Alumni Facebook Page

"Let us go forward in peace, our eyes upon heaven,
the only one goal of our labors."
~ St. Thérèse ~